D1387006

The Tempest (Study Guide)

The Tempest - A William Shakespeare Play, with Study Guide

(Literature Unpacked)

Eleanor Henderson

INTRODUCTION

Over the centuries, William Shakespeare's "The Tempest" has invited some criticism, both positive and negative. The play reflects prevailing attitudes of Shakespeare's time towards women and non-white people of colonized lands. Yet "The Tempest" is still considered to be one of Shakespeare's finer works, for he fills it with the most poetic language he has ever crafted. He also experiments with dramaturgy, in an attempt to blur the difference between reality and illusion.

PLOT SUMMARY

Prospero, the former Duke of Milan who now lives on a deserted island with his only daughter Miranda, sees an opportunity to regain his dukedom when he spots the ship of the Duke of Naples sailing past. Using his knowledge of the magic arts, he commands invisible spirits to aid him and conjures up a storm to wreck the ship and bring its passengers to shore, alive.

The passengers include not only Prospero's old rival, Alonso the Duke of Naples, and his son Ferdinand, but also Prospero's own brother Antonio, who had usurped the dukedom from Prospero and sent him adrift on a boat to exile. With the help of Ariel, a spirit, Prospero draws Ferdinand away from the rest of the party, to go wandering around the island.

After walking around, Ferdinand comes upon Miranda and fall in love with her. Miranda falls in love with him as well. This is all in keeping with Prospero's secret plan for them; but he pretends to be offended by Ferdinand's presence and makes him a prisoner-servant.

The rest of the shipwrecked party wander about in the island, and each of them soon begins to show their true motives. As Alonso wonders where Ferdinand is, his brother Sebastian and the ever-scheming Antonio plot to kill him in his sleep. The invisible Ariel comes to foil their plans by keeping old Gonzalo and the rest of the nobles awake.

And on another part of the island, the royal

party's inebriated butler and jester, Stephano and Trinculo, have been separated from the rest as well, and they begin to think they are the only survivors. They come upon Caliban, Prospero's vengeful half-human servant, who invites them to help him kill Prospero and take over the island. Stephano and Trinculo agree to do so. But Ariel has overheard everything.

With the help of Ariel's magic, Prospero has Trinculo, Stephano, and Caliban lose their way in the wilds of the island. And then Alonso, Antonio, Sebastian, Gonzalo and the others are led into a spot on the island where Ariel and other spirits prepare a lavish banquet for them – only to magically remove it from them as soon as they try to eat, as punishment for their treatment of Prospero. Alonso, Antonio, and Sebastian become despondent with guilt and regret over their past actions.

Meanwhile, Miranda goes to the enslaved Ferdinand, and they exchange vows of love. Convinced that their love is real, Prospero finally decides that everyone has suffered enough. He blessed Miranda and Ferdinand's union, and then has Ariel draw the rest of the shipwrecked party together before him for the first time. He then reveals himself and forgives those who tried to harm him. Alonso accepts Ferdinand and Miranda's marriage, and peace with Milan. Prospero is restored as Duke of Milan, and he and Miranda return home aboard the magically-restored ship together with the rest of the party. Prospero renounces his use of magic, and frees both Ariel and Caliban from his service. Only Caliban is left to live on the island.

CHARACTERS

"The Tempest" actually has 18 speaking parts, both major and minor characters, plus an unspecified number of mostly non-speaking extras playing sailors, nymphs, reapers, spirits and other fantastic creatures. We will focus only on the most important major and minor characters here.

Important Major Characters

Prospero

The exiled Duke of Milan is, as the title of the play suggests, a tempestuous man. Ever since his brother betrayed him, he has been battling bitterness and anger within himself. His moods and his temper are somewhat unpredictable, and we never really know if he plans to exact revenge until the end. But he overcomes his own private demons, shows the goodness hidden in his heart, and forgives those who have wronged him.

Miranda

Prospero's daughter is beautiful and innocent. She has led an extremely sheltered life, and she is devoted and obedient to her father. For most of the play, Miranda is the sole beacon of femininity and mercy. But her curiosity about the world outside of the island makes her question his actions. She tries to appease her father, even as she goes against (what she thinks are) his wishes and acts on her feelings for the prisoner Ferdinand.

Ariel

Ariel is not human but a spirit of the air and the elements, imbued with intelligence and a generally friendly nature. By following Prospero's orders to the letter, Ariel becomes, in effect, an extension of Prospero's will.

Alonso

Prior to getting shipwrecked on Prospero's deserted isle, Alonso was the sort of man who prioritized political gain above all else. His experience on the island changes his outlook in life.

Ferdinand

Alonso's only son is exactly like Miranda: he has led a sheltered life under his father's watchful eye, having known no other world except the royal court. He falls in love with Miranda the moment he sees her, and becomes willing to live as a servant just to be with her.

Antonio

Power-hungry, Antonio has no qualms about usurping his own brother from the dukedom, nor of getting rid of his ally, the Duke of Naples. Yet it is possible that he has a sliver of conscience. Instead of having Prospero and the infant Miranda hunted and assassinated, Antonio is content to have them leave Milan. He regrets his actions much later, when he is shipwrecked and hungry.

Sebastian

He is a man who is easily persuaded into anything, even to grabbing the reins of power from his own brother, the Duke of Naples. But he is exactly like Antonio, and his evil thoughts dissolve when frightened and chastised (by Ariel as a harpy).

Caliban

He is a deformed, seemingly half-human savage who was the sole sentient living being on the island before Prospero and Miranda arrived. Abandoned by his mother, he has no empathy for anyone else, much less gratitude to Prospero for having tried to educate him. Caliban is motivated only by self-centered desires – like his desire to torment other creatures and gain control over the island. He wants revenge over

Prospero above all, for turning him into a slave after trying to rape Miranda.

Important Minor Characters

Gonzalo – He is the old Milanese nobleman who tried to help Prospero and Miranda survive by stocking their boat with all the supplies needed for them to live elsewhere. He is kind-hearted, but he talks too much at times.

Trinculo and Stephano – Alonso's court jester and butler, respectively. After getting shipwrecked on Prospero's island, they lose all inhibitions, drink whatever alcohol they can find, and behave badly. They also plot to take over the island and kidnap Miranda.

HISTORICAL CONTEXT

"The Tempest" is believed to have been written sometime between the years 1610 to 1611, during the final years of William Shakespeare's active years in London theatre. It's also very likely the last play that Shakespeare wrote by himself, before retiring. Thus, the play not only reflects the social mores and prevailing styles of the day, but the life and maturity of William Shakespeare's skill as an older dramatist.

The romance plays

Shakespeare was around 46 years old when he wrote "The Tempest." By this time he was considered one of the more senior dramatists of England. It was also during this time that he started mentoring younger playwrights.

His mentorship took the form of collaborations with the likes of George Wilkins, Thomas Middleton, and John Fletcher.

But while he collaborated with them, Shakespeare was open to learning from the younger playwrights as well, incorporating some of their own ideas into his own plays.

This time in his career is called his "romantic period" because he created his romance plays – "Cymbeline", "The Winter's Tale", and "The Tempest". These works follow the formula of the tragicomedy, which were also called "romances." While the roots of this formula date back to ancient Greek theatre, it was first introduced to English theatre by John Fletcher.

Another influence on Shakespeare's romantic period was the masque. A masque was a scripted pageantry and a form of entertainment at the court of then current King of England, James I. These shows were part dance, part costume show, part performance art, featuring lavish costumes, choreography, and magnificent symbolic tableaus. Shakespeare's contemporary, the dramatist Ben Jonson, and architect Inigo Jones, were responsible for the staging of such performances at James I's court.

These influences can all be seen in how "The Tempest" is written. The beginning presents its protagonists suffering a tragic situation. But it all ends happily, with forgiveness and reconciliation. Along the way, the story features plenty of magic and fantastic creatures. The playful use of time, place, and action imbue the play with a "mystical" feel, similar to the fashionable courtly masques.

These scenes called for stage effects, props, and costumes, and more actors to help simulate sea storms, verdant forests, animals, monsters, and dancing spirits. This meant that staging them required the patronage of the wealthy nobility.

Jacobean beliefs

Shakespeare's life and career straddled the reigns of Queen Elizabeth I (1558-1603) and James I (1603 -1625). He was involved with the Lord Chamberlain's Men, an acting company with core members or "sharers" that included the likes of Richard Burbage and William Kempe. The company performed regularly in Queen Elizabeth's court.

As soon as the Queen died in 1603 and King James I ascended the English throne, the Lord Chamberlain's Men lost no time in getting the approval for their name to be changed to the "King's Men." This meant they officially had direct patronage of the King himself. But it also meant that the acting company – and Shakespeare himself – would have to cater to the King's tastes and interests.

Both Queen Elizabeth and King James were Protestant and shared certain political policies. But James I differed from Elizabeth I in his depth of interest in religion and magic.

King James was a talented scholar who dedicated himself to poetry and a somewhat

Puritan-influenced version of Protestantism. And he believed in the existence of magic, witches, and demons. When he was still James VI of Scotland, he had published his own book called "Daemonologie," a philosophical dissertation on magic, witchcraft, sorcery, and the classification of demons. He even participated in witch hunts and trials (like the trials at North Bernwick in 1590). And during his reign in England, he brought in this outlook as well: he famously sponsored the English translation of the Bible now called the Authorized King James Version.

King James's idea of Christianity also incorporated ideas that supported his rule. James believed in the divine right of kings to rule a nation with absolute authority, because they were ordained by God – and, in the case of James, as represented by the Church of England.

Defining virtues and vices from the English Protestant view was also tinged with colonialism and patriarchy.

Under James's rule, Great Britain (the combined kingdoms of Scotland and England) began the colonization of Americas in Virginia in 1607. So patriotism and religious fervor included a belief in Britain's right to conquer other lands and subdue the (non-white) natives, whom they believed to be inferior, and in need of tutelage and Christianization.

And as in times past, patriarchy infused all aspects of British culture and religion. So the monarch and all his most powerful nobles were first in the land, followed by the minor nobles, Protestant clergy, and the landed gentry. The common folk, peasants, women and resident foreigners were second-class citizens who had to conform to the rules and expectations imposed on them by the more dominant few.

Thus, the plays that King James and his court favored more of the tragicomedies of romances, which companies like the King's Men staged. With their opulent costumes and stage effects, such plays made awe-inspiring propaganda for the King's ideas on religion and the divine right of kings.

Thus, in "The Tempest" the villains are those who usurp the divine right of kings and the rules of proper succession. Vices and evil are associated with more common folk (like

Trinculo and Stephano), and "savages" (like Caliban) who are not of the same race or stock as the protagonists. The heroes of the story are often members of the nobility (as with Prospero, Ferdinand, and Gonzalo). And the few human female characters that are present (like Miranda) are chaste, fair-skinned, and happily subordinate to their fathers. (Even the female goddesses Iris, Ceres, and Juno, are reduced to being spirits seemingly in service to Prospero, Miranda's father.)

Retirement

Shakespeare retired soon after writing "The Tempest," to his hometown of Stratford-upon-Avon. At the time he retired, a middle-class, non-titled commoner going into full retirement from his career was practically unheard of. Very few men of his economic status could afford to do so.

But Shakespeare was both a lucky and shrewd man. Apart from having the good fortune to develop his playwriting skill and earn profits from the popularity of his plays in his own lifetime, he invested his money into real estate property purchases.

These purchases were made just years before his retirement, and included the land on which Shakespeare and his fellow theatre company members built the famous Globe Theater, and the Blackfriars Theater, where they held their winter productions. But more importantly, Shakespeare was able to purchase the second-largest home in Stratford (called New Place) and a share in the parish tithes. This home, and his earnings from the tithes, would ensure him a regular income for him, whether he continued to work in theater or not.

This meant financial security and some artistic freedom for Shakespeare. And since he was connected with the King's Men and had the backing of the King himself, he could envision and write such fanciful scenes for "The Tempest," such as the banquet dance for Duke Alonso and his entourage.

Notice, too, that nearly all of the important male characters in "The Tempest" can – or should – be played by middle-aged or old men (with the exception being Ferdinand, Adrian, and the mariners). Many of the major actors in the King's Men were Shakespeare's contemporaries, and the playwright had to create a story to suit their age.

It has also been suggested that the character of Prospero is something of an alter-ego for Shakespeare himself. The epilogue that Prospero recites certainly sounds like something an aging playwright would say of himself, with death in the horizon.

Shakespeare died on April 23, 1616, at the age of 52 – just five years after he finished writing "The Tempest".

THEMES

Being one of Shakespeare's fanciful romance plays, themes in "The Tempest" are more readily discerned in its poetic and visual language.

Magic and justice

In Jacobean England, magic was Satan's work, and it was an evil thing to believe and dabble in – even as people (especially King James himself) paradoxically believed in its existence and power. Magic was around, and it had to be stamped out in the name of Christianity.

Yet there's plenty of magic in "The Tempest," and it emanates from Prospero. Shakespeare works around the Jacobean paradox of believing and abhorring magic, by making Prospero use the dark magic arts to bring justice into the world, which primarily meant his restoration as Duke of Milan.

Shakespeare purposely describes Prospero's magic as a rational art, akin to how people in his day envisioned the study of science to be. Prospero speaks of himself as being "without parallel" in the study of the "liberal arts." Prospero's skill in magic is the result of careful intellectual study, with the help of precious books containing knowledge which he prized "above my dukedom."

Prospero's approach and use of magic is supposed to be different from that of the oft-mentioned witch Sycorax. While Prospero's magic is born out of rationality, Sycorax's knowledge of magic is born out of occultism and her worship of the devil. So, though her powers were terrible and destructive, they were limited. She was thus unable to command benevolent spirits such as Ariel to do her bidding. But Prospero, with his rationality and goodness, could engage the likes of Ariel.

Essentially, both Prospero and Sycorax used magic to gain power for their own purposes. We can thus look at the use of magic in "The Tempest" as an allegory for the propaganda and other political tricks that leaders use to maneuver their way into power. And whether they do this to bring justice and empowerment to the weak, or to simply empower themselves, their methods look almost alike. And, as if to underline the contentious nature of Prospero's magic,

Shakespeare inserts near the end of the play a little scene of Miranda and Ferdinand playing a game of chess. The young couple are so engrossed in their game that they do not immediately notice the arrival of Prospero, Alonso, and the others. They are only innocent political pawns of Prospero, and are oblivious to his magical machination.

But Shakespeare gives us a "happy" ending to all this. This is because the politician who prevails is Prospero, whose goals are presented as benevolent. He merely wants justice: the restoration of the proper order where he is the rightful Duke of Milan, where peace between Milan and Naples is achieved with the marriage between Ferdinand and the obedient daughter Miranda, where the usurping brothers

Antonio and Sebastian are properly chastised and forgiven, and unruly peasant subjects and colonized savages are subjugated. This is the "proper order" according to Jacobean ideals.

The human soul

What makes a human being human?

In "The Tempest", this question seems to be implied the most each time Caliban is in the scene. Caliban speaks and interacts with the other characters like any human being does. His vengeful thoughts are filled with as much treachery as what the likes of Trinculo, Stephano, Sebastian, and Prospero's own brother Antonio think of. And yet it is Caliban whose physical form is clearly deformed and not quite human. The other characters that interact with him do not think of him as human. So what's the difference between Caliban and the villainous humans in the story?

In Shakespeare's day, people thought of the answer to this question in terms of the Renaissance concept of the human being: an intelligent being with a body and soul. And that soul would have three aspects to it: the vegetative, the sensitive, and the rational. A human being is not one if he does not have a tripartite soul such as this. The "vegetative" is supposed to be the most basic aspect of the soul, and is about the basic needs for growth and reproduction. The "sensitive" is the aspect that involves motion, the senses, and reacting to the world. And the "rational" aspect covers sentient thought, introspection, and reflection.

This Renaissance idea about the tripartite human soul is echoed in Austrian Sigmund Freud's more modern interpretation of human psychology. Freud's model of the human psyche has three parts: the id, the ego, the super-ego. The id is the part of the psyche that is made up of bodily needs and desires – like hunger for food, safety, and sex – and is similar to the Renaissance concept of the "sensitive" and "vegetative" aspects of the soul. The ego is the sense of self, and is responsible for perceiving the world and making judgements for self-preservation and growth. And the super-ego is, in essence, a person's conscience or higher thought, which is supposed to guide and regulate the id and ego.

Notwithstanding the inherent bigotry in

having "The Tempest" villain be a deformed non-European, we can still look on the character of Caliban as an example of someone without a proper conscience – no super-ego or rational aspect – and therefore is not completely human.

In that sense, Alonso, Antonio, and Sebastian are like Caliban. They had plotted against Prospero in the past, usurping his power and ignoring what their consciences very likely bid them not to do. It was as if they had no consciences at all. Thus, when they arrive at Prospero's island and behold the magical banquet that Ariel lays out, Ariel calls them "three men of sin" who are "unfit to live" and must not be counted among human beings.

The difference between the less-than-human

maybe Caliban doesn't have a conscience

n and the three nobles lies in their

n to chastisement. When Prospero chastises Caliban for trying to rape Miranda in the past, Caliban cowers before him out of fear, instead of learning to care for Miranda's welfare. But after Ariel chastises the three nobles, it awakens their consciences and they feel monstrous guilt over what they had done to Prospero in the past. They become fully human once again.

Reality versus illusion

Shakespeare has toyed with different layers of reality before in earlier-written plays – for instance, the play-within-a-play for "Hamlet" and the interlocking worlds of the fairies, the humans, and stage play for "A Midsummer Night's Dream."

But in "The Tempest," Shakespeare tries to blur reality and illusion a little further.

Prospero is like the master of a puppet show, where he pulls all the strings that control the movements and reactions of the other characters. With the help of Ariel and the other spirits he has enthralled, Prospero can make other people go where he wishes, see only what he wants them to see, make them asleep or awake at the right time, and prevent them from moving at any given time. He even manipulates his own daughter Miranda and her would-be husband Ferdinand, throwing them both false hurdles and incentives to end up in each other's arms. Everyone's perception of reality is at Prospero's mercy; even the spirits obey him. Only Prospero has full control over himself.

Or does he? The literal sea storm that Prospero conjures up in the beginning seems like a manifestation of his own deep-seated rage at being betrayed by his own brother. The tempest ceases only when Prospero is satisfied that his plans are being fulfilled.

Also, Prospero's servants, Caliban and Ariel, are such polar oppositesthat, standing next to Prospero, a comparison of them to the concepts of id (Caliban), ego (Prospero) and super-ego (Ariel) is easily made. Perhaps all of Propero's art is not really magic but a manifestation of his psyche. But then it invites the question: how much of reality and of himself does Prospero really control?

But Shakespeare saves the best of the reality-blurring for last.

In Act 4, Prospero begins to reveal his workings on the other characters of the play. He says to Ferdinand, "Our revels now are ended. These our actors, as I foretold you, were all spirits and are melted into... thin air." He further adds: "We are such stuff as dreams are made on, and our little life is rounded with a sleep." In short, he reminds Ferdinand that man's existence could be considered as like a dream in God's mind.

And then, in the epilogue, after all that magic provides Prospero with the happy ending he seeks, he suddenly breaks the fourth wall and speaks to the audience.

"Now my charms are all o'erthrown," Prospero says to the audience. "Now 'tis true, I must be here confined by you, or sent to Naples." Then he begs to be pardoned for being the deceiver, and to be released from the spell that keeps him on the island, with the audience's help. "Let your indulgence set me free."

This is a fictional character, saying that his fate rests on how the audience will imagine the rest of the happy ending to be, beyond written ending of the play. Prospero is admitting he is also under the magic spell of the audience. And like Ariel, he seeks his freedom from it. The audience then can wonder how much of their own lives are also a "dream."

KEY SCENES & IMPORTANT QUOTES

"The Tempest" is filled with beautiful and memorable lines. Here are a few important quotes that capture the essence of the story and themes perfectly.

1. **"But how is it that this lives in thy mind?   What seest thou else   In the dark backward and abysm of time?"   - Prospero**

(From Act 1 Scene 2.) Shakespeare provides this haunting description of the nature of memory and time during Prospero's conversation with his daughter Miranda, as they reminisce on how they first got to live on the island.

2. "[There's nothing ill can dwell in such a temple.

If the ill spirit have so fair a house,

Good things will strive to dwell with't." - Miranda

(From Act 1, Scene 2.) This is Miranda's flattering description of Ferdinand's appearance.

3. "Full fathom five thy father lies;

Of his bones are coral made;

Those are pearls that were his eyes:

Nothing of him that doth fade

But doth suffer a sea-change

Into something rich and strange.

Sea-nymphs hourly ring his knell..." - Ariel

(From Act 1, Scene 2.) These are the words to

the song that the invisible Ariel sings into the astonished Ferdinand's ear as he searches the island for his father Alonso.

4. "Misery acquaints a man with strange bedfellows." - Trinculo

(From Act 2, Scene 2.) Trinculo is a court jester who came along with Duke Alonso's party aboard the ship. He is a fool, yet out of his mouth comes the wisest of sayings, like this one about the desperation of man.

5. "We are such stuff
As dreams are made on; and our little life
Is rounded with a sleep."   - Prospero

(From Act 4, Scene 1.) Shakespeare gives this succinct description of a philosophical idea about the nature of reality being like a dream. This line forms part of Prospero's speech to Ferdinand about his perception of the nature of the island – and of life itself.

6. "How many goodly creatures are there here!

How beauteous mankind is! O brave new world

That has such people in't!" - Miranda

(From Act 5, Scene 1.) Despite Prospero's somewhat bleak description of life being a fleeting dream of sorts, Miranda still revels and believes in the world's beauty.

SUGGESTED STUDY

Here are a few extra topics you can explore on your own, or use for any essay or analysis your teacher may ask you to write.

1. Miranda

Miranda is the typical stage play heroine of that time: fair, chaste, passive and obedient. She is there to be Prospero's pawn in his virtual game of chess. Or is she? Look closely to how she conducts herself around her father, Prospero, and Ferdinand. Is she actually rebellious in her own way? Why or why not? And how does she compare to our ideas today of what fictional heroines are supposed to be like in stories?

2. Justifiying the means

Would you say that the manner in which Prospero regained his power was justified? Was it fair for him to manipulate the others so thoroughly, just to get what he wanted? Why do you think Prospero thought giving his brother and Alonso a chance to repent was a good idea? What would you have done in Prospero's place, had you the same magic powers? Why?

THE TEMPEST

William Shakespeare. 1612.

Table Of Contents

DRAMATIS PERSONAE

ALONSO, King of Naples

SEBASTIAN, his brother

PROSPERO, the right Duke of Milan

ANTONIO, his brother, the usurping Duke of Milan

FERDINAND, son to the King of Naples

GONZALO, an honest old counsellor

Lords

ADRIAN

FRANCISCO

CALIBAN, a savage and deformed slave

TRINCULO, a jester

STEPHANO, a drunken butler

MASTER OF A SHIP

BOATSWAIN

MARINERS

MIRANDA, daughter to Prospero

ARIEL, an airy spirit

Spirits

IRIS

CERES

JUNO

NYMPHS

REAPERS

Other Spirits attending on Prospero

SCENE: A ship at sea; afterwards an uninhabited island

ACT I. SCENE 1

On a ship at sea; a tempestuous noise of thunder and lightning heard

Enter a SHIPMASTER and a BOATSWAIN

MASTER. Boatswain!

BOATSWAIN. Here, master; what cheer?

MASTER. Good! Speak to th' mariners; fall to't yarely, or we run ourselves aground; bestir, bestir.

Exit

Enter MARINERS

BOATSWAIN. Heigh, my hearts! cheerly, cheerly, my hearts! yare, yare! Take in the topsail. Tend to th' master's whistle. Blow till thou burst thy wind, if room enough.

Enter ALONSO, SEBASTIAN, ANTONIO, FERDINAND GONZALO, and OTHERS

ALONSO. Good boatswain, have care. Where's the master?

Play the men.

BOATSWAIN. I pray now, keep below.

ANTONIO. Where is the master, boson?

BOATSWAIN. Do you not hear him? You mar our labour;

keep your cabins; you do assist the storm.

GONZALO. Nay, good, be patient.

BOATSWAIN. When the sea is. Hence! What cares these roarers for the name of king? To cabin! silence! Trouble us not.

GONZALO. Good, yet remember whom thou hast aboard.

BOATSWAIN. None that I more love than myself. You are counsellor; if you can command these elements to silence, and work the peace of the present, we will not hand a rope more. Use your authority; if you cannot, give thanks you have liv'd so long, and make yourself read in your cabin for the mischance of the hour, if it so hap.-Cheerly, good hearts!- Out of our way, I say.

Exit

GONZALO. I have great comfort from this fellow. Methinks he hath no drowning mark upon him; his complexion is perfect gallows. Stand fast, good Fate, to his hanging; make the rope of his destiny our cable, for our own doth little advantage. If he be not born to be ng'd, our case is miserable.

Exeunt

Re-enter BOATSWAIN

BOATSWAIN. Down with the topmast. Yare, lower, lower!

Bring her to try wi' th' maincourse. [A cry within] A plague upon this howling! They are louder than the weather or our office.

Re-enter SEBASTIAN, ANTONIO, and GONZALO

Yet again! What do you here? Shall we give o'er, and drown? Have you a mind to sink?

SEBASTIAN. A pox o' your throat, you bawling, blasphemous, incharitable dog!

BOATSWAIN. Work you, then.

ANTONIO. Hang, cur; hang, you whoreson, insolent noisemaker; we are less afraid to be drown'd than thou art.

GONZALO. I'll warrant him for drowning, though the ship were no stronger than a nutshell, and as leaky as an unstanched wench.

BOATSWAIN. Lay her a-hold, a-hold; set her two courses; off to sea again; lay her off.

Enter MARINERS, Wet MARINERS. All lost! to prayers, to prayers! all lost!

Exeunt

BOATSWAIN. What, must our mouths be cold?

GONZALO. The King and Prince at prayers!

Let's assist them,

For our case is as theirs.

SEBASTIAN. I am out of patience.

ANTONIO. We are merely cheated of our lives by drunkards.

This wide-chopp'd rascal-would thou mightst lie drowning

The washing of ten tides!

GONZALO. He'll be hang'd yet,

Though every drop of water swear against it,

And gape at wid'st to glut him.

[A confused noise within: Mercy on us!

We split, we split! Farewell, my wife and children!

Farewell, brother! We split, we split, we split!]

ANTONIO. Let's all sink wi' th' King.

SEBASTIAN. Let's take leave of him.

Exeunt ANTONIO and SEBASTIAN

GONZALO. Now would I give a thousand furlongs of sea for an acre of barren ground- long heath, brown furze, any thing. The wills above be done, but I would fain die dry death.

Exeunt

SCENE 2

The Island. Before PROSPERO'S cell

Enter PROSPERO and MIRANDA

MIRANDA. If by your art, my dearest father, you have
Put the wild waters in this roar, allay them.
The sky, it seems, would pour down stinking pitch,
But that the sea, mounting to th' welkin's cheek,
Dashes the fire out. O, I have suffered
With those that I saw suffer! A brave vessel,
Who had no doubt some noble creature in her,
Dash'd all to pieces! O, the cry did knock

Against my very heart! Poor souls, they perish'd.

Had I been any god of power, I would

Have sunk the sea within the earth or ere

It should the good ship so have swallow'd and

The fraughting souls within her.

PROSPERO. Be conected;

No more amazement; tell your piteous heart

There's no harm done.

MIRANDA. O, woe the day!

PROSPERO. No harm.

I have done nothing but in care of thee,

Of thee, my dear one, thee, my daughter, who

Art ignorant of what thou art, nought knowing

Of whence I am, nor that I am more better

Than Prospero, master of a full poor cell,

And thy no greater father.

MIRANDA. More to know

Did never meddle with my thoughts.

PROSPERO. 'Tis time

I should inform thee farther. Lend thy hand,

And pluck my magic garment from me. So,

[Lays down his mantle]

Lie there my art. Wipe thou thine eyes; have

comfort.

The direful spectacle of the wreck, which

touch'd

The very virtue of compassion in thee,

I have with such provision in mine art

So safely ordered that there is no soul-

No, not so much perdition as an hair

Betid to any creature in the vessel

Which thou heard'st cry, which thou saw'st

sink.

Sit down, for thou must now know farther.

MIRANDA. You have often

Begun to tell me what I am; but stopp'd,

And left me to a bootless inquisition,

  Concluding 'Stay; not yet.'

 PROSPERO. The hour's now come;

  The very minute bids thee ope thine ear.

  Obey, and be attentive. Canst thou remember

remember

  A time before we came unto this cell?

  I do not think thou canst; for then thou wast not

not

  Out three years old.

 MIRANDA. Certainly, sir, I can.

 PROSPERO. By what? By any other house, or person?

person?

  Of any thing the image, tell me, that

  Hath kept with thy remembrance?

 MIRANDA. 'Tis far off,

  And rather like a dream than an assurance

  That my remembrance warrants. Had I not

  Four, or five, women once, that tended me?

PROSPERO. Thou hadst, and more, Miranda. But how is it

That this lives in thy mind? What seest thou else

In the dark backward and abysm of time?

If thou rememb'rest aught, ere thou cam'st here,

How thou cam'st here thou mayst.

MIRANDA. But that I do not.

PROSPERO. Twelve year since, Miranda, twelve year since,

Thy father was the Duke of Milan, and

A prince of power.

MIRANDA. Sir, are not you my father?

PROSPERO. Thy mother was a piece of virtue, and

She said thou wast my daughter; and thy father

Was Duke of Milan, and his only heir

And princess no worse issued.

MIRANDA. O, the heavens!

What foul play had we that we came from thence?

Or blessed was't we did?

PROSPERO. Both, both, my girl.

By foul play, as thou say'st, were we heav'd thence;

But blessedly holp hither.

MIRANDA. O, my heart bleeds

To think o' th' teen that I have turn'd you to,

Which is from my remembrance. Please you, farther.

PROSPERO. My brother and thy uncle, call'd Antonio-

I pray thee, mark me that a brother should

Be so perfidious. He, whom next thyself

Of all the world I lov'd, and to him put

The manage of my state; as at that time

Through all the signories it was the first,

And Prospero the prime duke, being so reputed

In dignity, and for the liberal arts

Without a parallel, those being all my study-

The government I cast upon my brother

And to my state grew stranger, being transported

And rapt in secret studies. Thy false uncle-

Dost thou attend me?

MIRANDA. Sir, most heedfully.

PROSPERO. Being once perfected how to grant suits,

How to deny them, who t' advance, and who

To trash for over-topping, new created

The creatures that were mine, I say, or chang'd 'em,

Or else new form'd 'em; having both the key

Of officer and office, set all hearts i' th' state

To what tune pleas'd his ear; that now he was

The ivy which had hid my princely trunk

And suck'd my verdure out on't. Thou
attend'st not.

MIRANDA. O, good sir, I do!

PROSPERO. I pray thee, mark me.

I thus neglecting worldly ends, all dedicated

To closeness and the bettering of my mind

With that which, but by being so retir'd,

O'er-priz'd all popular rate, in my false
brother

Awak'd an evil nature; and my trust,

Like a good parent, did beget of him

A falsehood, in its contrary as great

As my trust was; which had indeed no limit,

A confidence sans bound. He being thus
lorded,

Not only with what my revenue yielded,

But what my power might else exact, like
one

Who having into truth, by telling of it,

Made such a sinner of his memory,

To credit his own lie-he did believe

He was indeed the Duke; out o' th'

substitution,

And executing th' outward face of royalty

With all prerogative. Hence his ambition

growing-

Dost thou hear?

MIRANDA. Your tale, sir, would cure deafness.

PROSPERO. To have no screen between this

part he play'd

And him he play'd it for, he needs will be

Absolute Milan. Me, poor man-my library

Was dukedom large enough-of temporal

royalties

He thinks me now incapable; confederates,

So dry he was for sway, wi' th' King of

Naples,

To give him annual tribute, do him homage,

Subject his coronet to his crown, and bend

The dukedom, yet unbow'd-alas, poor
Milan!-

To most ignoble stooping.

MIRANDA. O the heavens!

PROSPERO. Mark his condition, and th' event,
then tell me

If this might be a brother.

MIRANDA. I should sin

To think but nobly of my grandmother:

Good wombs have borne bad sons.

PROSPERO. Now the condition:

This King of Naples, being an enemy

To me inveterate, hearkens my brother's
suit;

Which was, that he, in lieu o' th' premises,

Of homage, and I know not how much
tribute,

Should presently extirpate me and mine

Out of the dukedom, and confer fair Milan

With all the honours on my brother. Whereon,

A treacherous army levied, one midnight

Fated to th' purpose, did Antonio open

The gates of Milan; and, i' th' dead of darkness,

The ministers for th' purpose hurried thence

Me and thy crying self.

MIRANDA. Alack, for pity!

I, not rememb'ring how I cried out then,

Will cry it o'er again; it is a hint

That wrings mine eyes to't.

PROSPERO. Hear a little further,

And then I'll bring thee to the present busines

Which now's upon 's; without the which this story

Were most impertinent.

MIRANDA. Wherefore did they not

That hour destroy us?

PROSPERO. Well demanded, wench!

My tale provokes that question. Dear, they durst not,

So dear the love my people bore me; nor set

A mark so bloody on the business; but

With colours fairer painted their foul ends.

In few, they hurried us aboard a bark;

Bore us some leagues to sea, where they prepared

A rotten carcass of a butt, not rigg'd,

Nor tackle, sail, nor mast; the very rats

Instinctively have quit it. There they hoist us,

To cry to th' sea, that roar'd to us; to sigh

To th' winds, whose pity, sighing back again,

Did us but loving wrong.

MIRANDA. Alack, what trouble

Was I then to you!

PROSPERO. O, a cherubin

Thou wast that did preserve me! Thou didst smile,

Infused with a fortitude from heaven,

When I have deck'd the sea with drops full
salt,

Under my burden groan'd; which rais'd in
me

An undergoing stomach, to bear up

Against what should ensue.

MIRANDA. How came we ashore?

PROSPERO. By Providence divine.

Some food we had and some fresh water
that

A noble Neapolitan, Gonzalo,

Out of his charity, who being then appointed

Master of this design, did give us, with

Rich garments, linens, stuffs, and
necessaries,

Which since have steaded much; so, of his
gentleness,

Knowing I lov'd my books, he furnish'd me

From mine own library with volumes that

I prize above my dukedom.

MIRANDA. Would I might

But ever see that man!

PROSPERO. Now I arise.

[Puts on his mantle]

Sit still, and hear the last of our sea-sorrow.

Here in this island we arriv'd; and here

Have I, thy schoolmaster, made thee more

profit

Than other princess' can, that have more

time

For vainer hours, and tutors not so careful.

MIRANDA. Heavens thank you for't! And now,

I pray you,

sir,

For still 'tis beating in my mind, your reason

For raising this sea-storm?

PROSPERO. Know thus far forth:

By accident most strange, bountiful Fortune,

Now my dear lady, hath mine enemies

Brought to this shore; and by my prescience

I find my zenith doth depend upon

A most auspicious star, whose influence

If now I court not, but omit, my fortunes

Will ever after droop. Here cease more

questions;

Thou art inclin'd to sleep; 'tis a good

dullness,

And give it way. I know thou canst not

choose.

[MIRANDA sleeps]

Come away, servant; come; I am ready now.

Approach, my Ariel. Come.

Enter ARIEL

ARIEL. All hail, great master! grave sir, hail! I

come

To answer thy best pleasure; be't to fly,

To swim, to dive into the fire, to ride

On the curl'd clouds. To thy strong bidding task

Ariel and all his quality.

PROSPERO. Hast thou, spirit,

Perform'd to point the tempest that I bade thee?

ARIEL. To every article.

I boarded the King's ship; now on the beak,

Now in the waist, the deck, in every cabin,

I flam'd amazement. Sometime I'd divide,

And burn in many places; on the topmast,

The yards, and bowsprit, would I flame distinctly,

Then meet and join Jove's lightning, the precursors

O' th' dreadful thunder-claps, more momentary

And sight-outrunning were not; the fire and cracks

Of sulphurous roaring the most mighty Neptune

Seem to besiege, and make his bold waves tremble,

Yea, his dread trident shake.

PROSPERO. My brave spirit!

Who was so firm, so constant, that this coil

Would not infect his reason?

ARIEL. Not a soul

But felt a fever of the mad, and play'd

Some tricks of desperation. All but mariners

Plung'd in the foaming brine, and quit the vessel,

Then all afire with me; the King's son, Ferdinand,

With hair up-staring-then like reeds, not hair-

Was the first man that leapt; cried 'Hell is empty,

And all the devils are here.'

PROSPERO. Why, that's my spirit!

But was not this nigh shore?

ARIEL. Close by, my master.

PROSPERO. But are they, Ariel, safe?

ARIEL. Not a hair perish'd;

On their sustaining garments not a blemish,

But fresher than before; and, as thou bad'st me,

In troops I have dispers'd them 'bout the isle.

The King's son have I landed by himself,

Whom I left cooling of the air with sighs

In an odd angle of the isle, and sitting,

His arms in this sad knot.

PROSPERO. Of the King's ship,

The mariners, say how thou hast dispos'd,

And all the rest o' th' fleet?

ARIEL. Safely in harbour

Is the King's ship; in the deep nook, where once

Thou call'dst me up at midnight to fetch dew

From the still-vex'd Bermoothes, there she's

hid;

The mariners all under hatches stowed,

Who, with a charm join'd to their suff'red

labour,

I have left asleep; and for the rest o' th' fleet,

Which I dispers'd, they all have met again,

And are upon the Mediterranean flote

Bound sadly home for Naples,

Supposing that they saw the King's ship

wreck'd,

And his great person perish.

PROSPERO. Ariel, thy charge

Exactly is perform'd; but there's more work.

What is the time o' th' day?

ARIEL. Past the mid season.

PROSPERO. At least two glasses. The time

'twixt six and now

Must by us both be spent most preciously.

ARIEL. Is there more toil? Since thou dost give me pains,

Let me remember thee what thou hast promis'd,

Which is not yet perform'd me.

PROSPERO. How now, moody?

What is't thou canst demand?

ARIEL. My liberty.

PROSPERO. Before the time be out? No more!

ARIEL. I prithee,

Remember I have done thee worthy service,

Told thee no lies, made thee no mistakings, serv'd

Without or grudge or grumblings. Thou didst promise

To bate me a full year.

PROSPERO. Dost thou forget

From what a torment I did free thee?

ARIEL. No.

PROSPERO. Thou dost; and think'st it much to tread the ooze

Of the salt deep,

To run upon the sharp wind of the north,

To do me business in the veins o' th' earth

When it is bak'd with frost.

ARIEL. I do not, sir.

PROSPERO. Thou liest, malignant thing. Hast thou forgot

The foul witch Sycorax, who with age and envy

Was grown into a hoop? Hast thou forgot her?

ARIEL. No, sir.

PROSPERO. Thou hast. Where was she born? Speak; tell me.

ARIEL. Sir, in Argier.

PROSPERO. O, was she so? I must

Once in a month recount what thou hast been,

Which thou forget'st. This damn'd witch Sycorax,

For mischiefs manifold, and sorceries terrible

To enter human hearing, from Argier

Thou know'st was banish'd; for one thing she did

They would not take her life. Is not this true?

ARIEL. Ay, sir.

PROSPERO. This blue-ey'd hag was hither brought with child,

And here was left by th'sailors. Thou, my slave,

As thou report'st thyself, wast then her servant;

And, for thou wast a spirit too delicate

To act her earthy and abhorr'd commands,

Refusing her grand hests, she did confine thee,

By help of her more potent ministers,

And in her most unmitigable rage,

Into a cloven pine; within which rift

Imprison'd thou didst painfully remain

A dozen years; within which space she died,

And left thee there, where thou didst vent
thy groans

As fast as mill-wheels strike. Then was this
island-

Save for the son that she did litter here,

A freckl'd whelp, hag-born-not honour'd
with

A human shape.

ARIEL. Yes, Caliban her son.

PROSPERO. Dull thing, I say so; he, that
Caliban

Whom now I keep in service. Thou best
know'st

What torment I did find thee in; thy groans

Did make wolves howl, and penetrate the
breasts

Of ever-angry bears; it was a torment

To lay upon the damn'd, which Sycorax

Could not again undo. It was mine art,

When I arriv'd and heard thee, that made gape

The pine, and let thee out.

ARIEL. I thank thee, master.

PROSPERO. If thou more murmur'st, I will rend an oak

And peg thee in his knotty entrails, till

Thou hast howl'd away twelve winters.

ARIEL. Pardon, master;

I will be correspondent to command,

And do my spriting gently.

PROSPERO. Do so; and after two days

I will discharge thee.

ARIEL. That's my noble master!

What shall I do? Say what. What shall I do?

PROSPERO. Go make thyself like a nymph o'
th' sea; be subject

To no sight but thine and mine, invisible

To every eyeball else. Go take this shape,

And hither come in 't. Go, hence with

diligence!

Exit ARIEL

Awake, dear heart, awake; thou hast slept

well;

Awake.

MIRANDA. The strangeness of your story put

Heaviness in me.

PROSPERO. Shake it off. Come on,

We'll visit Caliban, my slave, who never

Yields us kind answer.

MIRANDA. 'Tis a villain, sir,

I do not love to look on.

PROSPERO. But as 'tis,

We cannot miss him: he does make our fire,

Fetch in our wood, and serves in offices

That profit us. What ho! slave! Caliban!

Thou earth, thou! Speak.

CALIBAN. [Within] There's wood enough within.

PROSPERO. Come forth, I say; there's other business for thee.

Come, thou tortoise! when?

Re-enter ARIEL like a water-nymph

Fine apparition! My quaint Ariel,
Hark in thine ear.

ARIEL. My lord, it shall be done.

Exit

PROSPERO. Thou poisonous slave, got by the devil himself

Upon thy wicked dam, come forth!

Enter CALIBAN

CALIBAN. As wicked dew as e'er my mother brush'd

With raven's feather from unwholesome fen

Drop on you both! A south-west blow on ye

And blister you all o'er!

  PROSPERO. For this, be sure, to-night thou

shalt have cramps,

  Side-stitches that shall pen thy breath up;

urchins

  Shall, for that vast of night that they may

work,

  All exercise on thee; thou shalt be pinch'd

  As thick as honeycomb, each pinch more

stinging

  Than bees that made 'em.

  CALIBAN. I must eat my dinner.

  This island's mine, by Sycorax my mother,

  Which thou tak'st from me. When thou

cam'st first,

  Thou strok'st me and made much of me,

wouldst give me

  Water with berries in't, and teach me how

To name the bigger light, and how the less,

That burn by day and night; and then I lov'd
thee,

And show'd thee all the qualities o' th' isle,

The fresh springs, brine-pits, barren place
and fertile.

Curs'd be I that did so! All the charms

Of Sycorax, toads, beetles, bats, light on you!

For I am all the subjects that you have,

Which first was mine own king; and here
you sty me

In this hard rock, whiles you do keep from
me

The rest o' th' island.

PROSPERO. Thou most lying slave,

Whom stripes may move, not kindness! I
have us'd thee,

Filth as thou art, with human care, and
lodg'd thee

In mine own cell, till thou didst seek to violate

The honour of my child.

CALIBAN. O ho, O ho! Would't had been done.

Thou didst prevent me; I had peopl'd else

This isle with Calibans.

MIRANDA. Abhorred slave,

Which any print of goodness wilt not take,

Being capable of all ill! I pitied thee,

Took pains to make thee speak, taught thee each hour

One thing or other. When thou didst not, savage,

Know thine own meaning, but wouldst gabble like

A thing most brutish, I endow'd thy purposes

With words that made them known. But thy vile race,

Though thou didst learn, had that in't which good natures

Could not abide to be with; therefore wast thou

Deservedly confin'd into this rock, who hadst

Deserv'd more than a prison.

CALIBAN. You taught me language, and my profit on't

Is, I know how to curse. The red plague rid you

For learning me your language!

PROSPERO. Hag-seed, hence!

Fetch us in fuel. And be quick, thou 'rt best,

To answer other business. Shrug'st thou, malice?

If thou neglect'st, or dost unwillingly

What I command, I'll rack thee with old cramps,

Fill all thy bones with aches, make thee roar,

That beasts shall tremble at thy din.

CALIBAN. No, pray thee.

[Aside] I must obey. His art is of such pow'r,

It would control my dam's god, Setebos,

And make a vassal of him.

PROSPERO. So, slave; hence!

Exit CALIBAN

Re-enter ARIEL invisible, playing ad
singing; FERDINAND following

ARIEL'S SONG.

Come unto these yellow sands,

And then take hands;

Curtsied when you have and kiss'd,

The wild waves whist,

Foot it featly here and there,

And, sweet sprites, the burden bear.

Hark, hark!

[Burden dispersedly: Bow-wow.]

The watch dogs bark.

[Burden dispersedly: Bow-wow.]

Hark, hark! I hear

The strain of strutting chanticleer

Cry, Cock-a-diddle-dow.

FERDINAND. Where should this music be? I'
th' air or th'

earth?

It sounds no more; and sure it waits upon

Some god o' th' island. Sitting on a bank,

Weeping again the King my father's wreck,

This music crept by me upon the waters,

Allaying both their fury and my passion

With its sweet air; thence I have follow'd it,

Or it hath drawn me rather. But 'tis gone.

No, it begins again.

ARIEL'S SONG

Full fathom five thy father lies;

Of his bones are coral made;

Those are pearls that were his eyes;

  Nothing of him that doth fade

But doth suffer a sea-change

Into something rich and strange.

Sea-nymphs hourly ring his knell:

  [Burden: Ding-dong.]

Hark! now I hear them-Ding-dong bell.

FERDINAND. The ditty does remember my
drown'd father.

  This is no mortal business, nor no sound

  That the earth owes. I hear it now above me.

PROSPERO. The fringed curtains of thine eye
advance,

  And say what thou seest yond.

MIRANDA. What is't? a spirit?

  Lord, how it looks about! Believe me, sir,

  It carries a brave form. But 'tis a spirit.

PROSPERO. No, wench; it eats and sleeps and
hath such senses

As we have, such. This gallant which thou seest

Was in the wreck; and but he's something stain'd

With grief, that's beauty's canker, thou mightst call him

A goodly person. He hath lost his fellows,

And strays about to find 'em.

MIRANDA. I might call him

A thing divine; for nothing natural

I ever saw so noble.

PROSPERO. [Aside] It goes on, I see,

As my soul prompts it. Spirit, fine spirit! I'll free thee

Within two days for this.

FERDINAND. Most sure, the goddess

On whom these airs attend! Vouchsafe my pray'r

May know if you remain upon this island;

And that you will some good instruction give

How I may bear me here. My prime request,

Which I do last pronounce, is, O you wonder!

If you be maid or no?

MIRANDA. No wonder, sir;

But certainly a maid.

FERDINAND. My language? Heavens!

I am the best of them that speak this speech,

Were I but where 'tis spoken.

PROSPERO. How? the best?

What wert thou, if the King of Naples heard

thee?

FERDINAND. A single thing, as I am now, that

wonders

To hear thee speak of Naples. He does hear

me;

And that he does I weep. Myself am Naples,

Who with mine eyes, never since at ebb,

beheld

The King my father wreck'd.

MIRANDA. Alack, for mercy!

FERDINAND. Yes, faith, and all his lords, the Duke of Milan

And his brave son being twain.

PROSPERO. [Aside] The Duke of Milan

And his more braver daughter could control thee,

If now 'twere fit to do't. At the first sight

They have chang'd eyes. Delicate Ariel,

I'll set thee free for this. [To FERDINAND] A word, good

sir;

I fear you have done yourself some wrong; a word.

MIRANDA. Why speaks my father so ungently? This

Is the third man that e'er I saw; the first

That e'er I sigh'd for. Pity move my father

To be inclin'd my way!

FERDINAND. O, if a virgin,

And your affection not gone forth, I'll make you

The Queen of Naples.

PROSPERO. Soft, Sir! one word more.

[Aside] They are both in either's pow'rs; but this swift

busines

I must uneasy make, lest too light winning

Make the prize light. [To FERDINAND] One word more; I

charge thee

That thou attend me; thou dost here usurp

The name thou ow'st not; and hast put thyself

Upon this island as a spy, to win it

From me, the lord on't.

FERDINAND. No, as I am a man.

MIRANDA. There's nothing ill can dwell in such a temple.

If the ill spirit have so fair a house,

Good things will strive to dwell with't.

PROSPERO. Follow me.

Speak not you for him; he's a traitor. Come;

I'll manacle thy neck and feet together.

Sea-water shalt thou drink; thy food shall be

The fresh-brook mussels, wither'd roots, and husks

Wherein the acorn cradled. Follow.

FERDINAND. No;

I will resist such entertainment till

Mine enemy has more power.

[He draws, and is charmed from moving]

MIRANDA. O dear father,

Make not too rash a trial of him, for

He's gentle, and not fearful.

PROSPERO. What, I say,

My foot my tutor? Put thy sword up, traitor;

Who mak'st a show but dar'st not strike, thy conscience

Is so possess'd with guilt. Come from thy
ward;

For I can here disarm thee with this stick

And make thy weapon drop.

MIRANDA. Beseech you, father!

PROSPERO. Hence! Hang not on my garments.

MIRANDA. Sir, have pity;

I'll be his surety.

PROSPERO. Silence! One word more

Shall make me chide thee, if not hate thee.
What!

An advocate for an impostor! hush!

Thou think'st there is no more such shapes
as he,

Having seen but him and Caliban. Foolish
wench!

To th' most of men this is a Caliban,

And they to him are angels.

MIRANDA. My affections

Are then most humble; I have no ambition

To see a goodlier man.

PROSPERO. Come on; obey.

Thy nerves are in their infancy again,

And have no vigour in them.

FERDINAND. So they are;

My spirits, as in a dream, are all bound up.

My father's loss, the weakness which I feel,

The wreck of all my friends, nor this man's threats

To whom I am subdu'd, are but light to me,

Might I but through my prison once a day

Behold this maid. All corners else o' th' earth

Let liberty make use of; space enough

Have I in such a prison.

PROSPERO. [Aside] It works. [To FERDINAND] Come on.-

Thou hast done well, fine Ariel! [To FERDINAND] Follow

me.

[To ARIEL] Hark what thou else shalt do me.

MIRANDA. Be of comfort;

My father's of a better nature, sir,

Than he appears by speech; this is unwonted

Which now came from him.

PROSPERO. [To ARIEL] Thou shalt be as free

As mountain winds; but then exactly do

All points of my command.

ARIEL. To th' syllable.

PROSPERO. [To FERDINAND] Come, follow.
[To MIRANDA]

Speak not for him.   *Exeunt*

ACT II. SCENE 1

Another part of the island

Enter ALONSO, SEBASTIAN, ANTONIO, GONZALO, ADRIAN, FRANCISCO, and OTHERS

  GONZALO. Beseech you, sir, be merry; you have cause,

   So have we all, of joy; for our escape

   Is much beyond our loss. Our hint of woe

   Is common; every day, some sailor's wife,

   The masters of some merchant, and the merchant,

   Have just our theme of woe; but for the miracle,

   I mean our preservation, few in millions

Can speak like us. Then wisely, good sir, weigh

Our sorrow with our comfort.

ALONSO. Prithee, peace.

SEBASTIAN. He receives comfort like cold porridge.

ANTONIO. The visitor will not give him o'er so.

SEBASTIAN. Look, he's winding up the watch of his wit; by and by it will strike.

GONZALO. Sir-

SEBASTIAN. One-Tell.

GONZALO. When every grief is entertain'd that's offer'd,

Comes to th' entertainer-

SEBASTIAN. A dollar.

GONZALO. Dolour comes to him, indeed; you have spoken truer than you purpos'd.

SEBASTIAN. You have taken it wiselier than I meant you should.

GONZALO. Therefore, my lord-

ANTONIO. Fie, what a spendthrift is he of his tongue!

ALONSO. I prithee, spare.

GONZALO. Well, I have done; but yet-

SEBASTIAN. He will be talking.

ANTONIO. Which, of he or Adrian, for a good wager, first

   begins to crow?

SEBASTIAN. The old cock.

ANTONIO. The cock'rel.

SEBASTIAN. Done. The wager?

ANTONIO. A laughter.

SEBASTIAN. A match!

ADRIAN. Though this island seem to be desert-

ANTONIO. Ha, ha, ha!

SEBASTIAN. So, you're paid.

ADRIAN. Uninhabitable, and almost inaccessible-

SEBASTIAN. Yet-

ADRIAN. Yet-

ANTONIO. He could not miss't.

ADRIAN. It must needs be of subtle, tender, and delicate temperance.

ANTONIO. Temperance was a delicate wench.

SEBASTIAN. Ay, and a subtle; as he most learnedly
  deliver'd.

ADRIAN. The air breathes upon us here most sweetly.

SEBASTIAN. As if it had lungs, and rotten ones.

ANTONIO. Or, as 'twere perfum'd by a fen.

GONZALO. Here is everything advantageous to life.

ANTONIO. True; save means to live.

SEBASTIAN. Of that there's none, or little.

GONZALO. How lush and lusty the grass looks! how green!

ANTONIO. The ground indeed is tawny.

SEBASTIAN. With an eye of green in't.

ANTONIO. He misses not much.

SEBASTIAN. No; he doth but mistake the truth totally.

GONZALO. But the rarity of it is, which is indeed almost beyond credit-

SEBASTIAN. As many vouch'd rarities are.

GONZALO. That our garments, being, as they were, drench'd in the sea, hold, notwithstanding, their freshness and glosses, being rather new-dy'd, than stain'd with salt water.

ANTONIO. If but one of his pockets could speak, would it not say he lies?

SEBASTIAN. Ay, or very falsely pocket up his report.

GONZALO. Methinks our garments are now as fresh as when we put them on first in Afric, at the marriage of the King's fair daughter Claribel to the King of Tunis.

SEBASTIAN. 'Twas a sweet marriage, and we prosper well in our return.

ADRIAN. Tunis was never grac'd before with such a paragon to their queen.

GONZALO. Not since widow Dido's time.

ANTONIO. Widow! a pox o' that! How came that 'widow' in? Widow Dido!

SEBASTIAN. What if he had said 'widower Aeneas' too?

Good Lord, how you take it!

ADRIAN. 'Widow Dido' said you? You make me study of that. She was of Carthage, not of Tunis.

GONZALO. This Tunis, sir, was Carthage.

ADRIAN. Carthage?

GONZALO. I assure you, Carthage.

ANTONIO. His word is more than the miraculous harp.

SEBASTIAN. He hath rais'd the wall, and houses too.

ANTONIO. What impossible matter will he make easy next?

SEBASTIAN. I think he will carry this island home in his pocket, and give it his son for an apple.

ANTONIO. And, sowing the kernels of it in the sea, bring forth more islands.

GONZALO. Ay.

ANTONIO. Why, in good time.

GONZALO. Sir, we were talking that our garments seem now as fresh as when we were at Tunis at the marriage of your daughter, who is now Queen.

ANTONIO. And the rarest that e'er came there.

SEBASTIAN. Bate, I beseech you, widow Dido.

ANTONIO. O, widow Dido! Ay, widow Dido.

GONZALO. Is not, sir, my doublet as fresh as
the first day I wore it? I mean, in a sort.

ANTONIO. That 'sort' was well fish'd for.

GONZALO. When I wore it at your daughter's
marriage?

ALONSO. You cram these words into mine
ears against

    The stomach of my sense. Would I had never

    Married my daughter there; for, coming
thence,

    My son is lost; and, in my rate, she too,

    Who is so far from Italy removed

    I ne'er again shall see her. O thou mine heir

    Of Naples and of Milan, what strange fish

    Hath made his meal on thee?

FRANCISCO. Sir, he may live;

    I saw him beat the surges under him,

    And ride upon their backs; he trod the water,

    Whose enmity he flung aside, and breasted

The surge most swoln that met him; his bold head

'Bove the contentious waves he kept, and oared

Himself with his good arms in lusty stroke

To th' shore, that o'er his wave-worn basis bowed,

As stooping to relieve him. I not doubt

He came alive to land.

ALONSO. No, no, he's gone.

SEBASTIAN. Sir, you may thank yourself for this great loss,

That would not bless our Europe with your daughter,

But rather lose her to an African;

Where she, at least, is banish'd from your eye,

Who hath cause to wet the grief on't.

ALONSO. Prithee, peace.

SEBASTIAN. You were kneel'd to, and importun'd otherwise

By all of us; and the fair soul herself

Weigh'd between loathness and obedience at

Which end o' th' beam should bow. We have lost your son,

I fear, for ever. Milan and Naples have

Moe widows in them of this business' making,

Than we bring men to comfort them;

The fault's your own.

ALONSO. So is the dear'st o' th' loss.

GONZALO. My lord Sebastian,

The truth you speak doth lack some gentleness,

And time to speak it in; you rub the sore,

When you should bring the plaster.

SEBASTIAN. Very well.

ANTONIO. And most chirurgeonly.

GONZALO. It is foul weather in us all, good sir,
  When you are cloudy.

SEBASTIAN. Foul weather?

ANTONIO. Very foul.

GONZALO. Had I plantation of this isle, my
lord-

ANTONIO. He'd sow 't with nettle-seed.

SEBASTIAN. Or docks, or mallows.

GONZALO. And were the king on't, what
would I do?

SEBASTIAN. Scape being drunk for want of
wine.

GONZALO. I' th' commonwealth I would by
contraries
  Execute all things; for no kind of traffic
  Would I admit; no name of magistrate;
  Letters should not be known; riches,
poverty,
  And use of service, none; contract,
succession,

Bourn, bound of land, tilth, vineyard, none;

No use of metal, corn, or wine, or oil;

No occupation; all men idle, all;

And women too, but innocent and pure;

No sovereignty-

SEBASTIAN. Yet he would be king on't.

ANTONIO. The latter end of his
commonwealth forgets the

beginning.

GONZALO. All things in common nature
should produce

Without sweat or endeavour. Treason,
felony,

Sword, pike, knife, gun, or need of any
engine,

Would I not have; but nature should bring
forth,

Of it own kind, all foison, all abundance,

To feed my innocent people.

SEBASTIAN. No marrying 'mong his subjects?

ANTONIO. None, man; all idle; whores and knaves.

GONZALO. I would with such perfection govern, sir,

  T' excel the golden age.

SEBASTIAN. Save his Majesty!

ANTONIO. Long live Gonzalo!

GONZALO. And-do you mark me, sir?

ALONSO. Prithee, no more; thou dost talk nothing to me.

GONZALO. I do well believe your Highness; and did it to minister occasion to these gentlemen, who are of such sensible and nimble lungs that they always use to laugh at nothing.

ANTONIO. 'Twas you we laugh'd at.

GONZALO. Who in this kind of merry fooling am nothing to you; so you may continue, and laugh at nothing still.

ANTONIO. What a blow was there given!

SEBASTIAN. An it had not fall'n flat-long.

GONZALO. You are gentlemen of brave mettle; you would lift the moon out of her sphere, if she would continue in it five weeks without changing.

Enter ARIEL, invisible, playing solemn music

SEBASTIAN. We would so, and then go a-bat-fowling.

ANTONIO. Nay, good my lord, be not angry.

GONZALO. No, I warrant you; I will not adventure my discretion so weakly. Will you laugh me asleep, for I am very heavy?

ANTONIO. Go sleep, and hear us.

[All sleep but ALONSO, SEBASTIAN and ANTONIO]

ALONSO. What, all so soon asleep! I wish mine eyes

Would, with themselves, shut up my
thoughts; I find

    They are inclin'd to do so.

  SEBASTIAN. Please you, sir,

    Do not omit the heavy offer of it:

    It seldom visits sorrow; when it doth,

    It is a comforter.

  ANTONIO. We two, my lord,

    Will guard your person while you take your
rest,

    And watch your safety.

  ALONSO. Thank you-wondrous heavy!

                [ALONSO sleeps. Exit ARIEL]

  SEBASTIAN. What a strange drowsiness
possesses them!

  ANTONIO. It is the quality o' th' climate.

  SEBASTIAN. Why

    Doth it not then our eyelids sink? I find not

    Myself dispos'd to sleep.

  ANTONIO. Nor I; my spirits are nimble.

They fell together all, as by consent;

They dropp'd, as by a thunder-stroke. What might,

might,

Worthy Sebastian? O, what might! No more!

And yet methinks I see it in thy face,

What thou shouldst be; th' occasion speaks thee; and

thee; and

My strong imagination sees a crown

Dropping upon thy head.

SEBASTIAN. What, art thou waking?

ANTONIO. Do you not hear me speak?

SEBASTIAN. I do; and surely

It is a sleepy language, and thou speak'st

Out of thy sleep. What is it thou didst say?

This is a strange repose, to be asleep

With eyes wide open; standing, speaking, moving,

moving,

And yet so fast asleep.

ANTONIO. Noble Sebastian,

Thou let'st thy fortune sleep-die rather; wink'st

Whiles thou art waking.

SEBASTIAN. Thou dost snore distinctly;

There's meaning in thy snores.

ANTONIO. I am more serious than my custom; you

Must be so too, if heed me; which to do

Trebles thee o'er.

SEBASTIAN. Well, I am standing water.

ANTONIO. I'll teach you how to flow.

SEBASTIAN. Do so: to ebb,

Hereditary sloth instructs me.

ANTONIO. O,

If you but knew how you the purpose cherish,

Whiles thus you mock it! how, in stripping it,

You more invest it! Ebbing men indeed,

Most often, do so near the bottom run

By their own fear or sloth.

SEBASTIAN. Prithee say on.

The setting of thine eye and cheek proclaim

A matter from thee; and a birth, indeed,

Which throes thee much to yield.

ANTONIO. Thus, sir:

Although this lord of weak remembrance, this

Who shall be of as little memory

When he is earth'd, hath here almost persuaded-

For he's a spirit of persuasion, only

Professes to persuade-the King his son's alive,

'Tis as impossible that he's undrown'd

As he that sleeps here swims.

SEBASTIAN. I have no hope

That he's undrown'd.

ANTONIO. O, out of that 'no hope'

What great hope have you! No hope that way is

Another way so high a hope, that even

Ambition cannot pierce a wink beyond,

But doubt discovery there. Will you grant
with me

That Ferdinand is drown'd?

SEBASTIAN. He's gone.

ANTONIO. Then tell me,

Who's the next heir of Naples?

SEBASTIAN. Claribel.

ANTONIO. She that is Queen of Tunis; she that
dwells

Ten leagues beyond man's life; she that from
Naples

Can have no note, unless the sun were post,

The Man i' th' Moon's too slow, till newborn
chins

Be rough and razorable; she that from whom

We all were sea-swallow'd, though some
cast again,

And by that destiny, to perform an act

Whereof what's past is prologue, what to come

In yours and my discharge.

SEBASTIAN. What stuff is this! How say you?

'Tis true, my brother's daughter's Queen of Tunis;

So is she heir of Naples; 'twixt which regions

There is some space.

ANTONIO. A space whose ev'ry cubit

Seems to cry out 'How shall that Claribel

Measure us back to Naples? Keep in Tunis,

And let Sebastian wake.' Say this were death

That now hath seiz'd them; why, they were no worse

Than now they are. There be that can rule Naples

As well as he that sleeps; lords that can prate

As amply and unnecessarily

As this Gonzalo; I myself could make

A chough of as deep chat. O, that you bore

The mind that I do! What a sleep were this

For your advancement! Do you understand
me?

SEBASTIAN. Methinks I do.

ANTONIO. And how does your content

Tender your own good fortune?

SEBASTIAN. I remember

You did supplant your brother Prospero.

ANTONIO. True.

And look how well my garments sit upon me,

Much feater than before. My brother's
servants

Were then my fellows; now they are my
men.

SEBASTIAN. But, for your conscience-

ANTONIO. Ay, sir; where lies that? If 'twere a
kibe,

'Twould put me to my slipper; but I feel not

This deity in my bosom; twenty consciences

That stand 'twixt me and Milan, candied be
they

And melt, ere they molest! Here lies your
brother,

No better than the earth he lies upon,

If he were that which now he's like-that's
dead;

Whom I with this obedient steel, three
inches of it,

Can lay to bed for ever; whiles you, doing
thus,

To the perpetual wink for aye might put

This ancient morsel, this Sir Prudence, who

Should not upbraid our course. For all the
rest,

They'll take suggestion as a cat laps milk;

They'll tell the clock to any business that

We say befits the hour.

SEBASTIAN. Thy case, dear friend,

Shall be my precedent; as thou got'st Milan,

I'll come by Naples. Draw thy sword. One
stroke

Shall free thee from the tribute which thou
payest;

And I the King shall love thee.

ANTONIO. Draw together;

And when I rear my hand, do you the like,

To fall it on Gonzalo.

SEBASTIAN. O, but one word.

[They talk apart]

Re-enter ARIEL, invisible, with music and
song

ARIEL. My master through his art foresees
the danger

That you, his friend, are in; and sends me
forth-

For else his project dies-to keep them living.

[Sings in GONZALO'S ear]

While you here do snoring lie,

Open-ey'd conspiracy

His time doth take.

If of life you keep a care,

Shake off slumber, and beware.

Awake, awake!

ANTONIO. Then let us both be sudden.

GONZALO. Now, good angels

Preserve the King!

[They wake]

ALONSO. Why, how now?-Ho, awake!-Why

are you drawn?

Wherefore this ghastly looking?

GONZALO. What's the matter?

SEBASTIAN. Whiles we stood here securing

your repose,

Even now, we heard a hollow burst of

bellowing

Like bulls, or rather lions; did't not wake
you?

It struck mine ear most terribly.

ALONSO. I heard nothing.

ANTONIO. O, 'twas a din to fright a monster's
ear,

To make an earthquake! Sure it was the roar
Of a whole herd of lions.

ALONSO. Heard you this, Gonzalo?

GONZALO. Upon mine honour, sir, I heard a
humming,

And that a strange one too, which did awake
me;

I shak'd you, sir, and cried; as mine eyes
open'd,

I saw their weapons drawn-there was a
noise,

That's verily. 'Tis best we stand upon our
guard,

Or that we quit this place. Let's draw our weapons.

ALONSO. Lead off this ground; and let's make further

    search

    For my poor son.

GONZALO. Heavens keep him from these beasts!

    For he is, sure, i' th' island.

ALONSO. Lead away.

ARIEL. Prospero my lord shall know what I have done;

    So, King, go safely on to seek thy son.

       Exeunt

SCENE 2

Another part of the island

Enter CALIBAN, with a burden of wood. A noise of thunder heard

CALIBAN. All the infections that the sun sucks up
From bogs, fens, flats, on Prosper fall, and make him
By inch-meal a disease! His spirits hear me,
And yet I needs must curse. But they'll nor pinch,
Fright me with urchin-shows, pitch me i' th' mire,
Nor lead me, like a firebrand, in the dark
Out of my way, unless he bid 'em; but
For every trifle are they set upon me;

Sometime like apes that mow and chatter at
me,
   And after bite me; then like hedgehogs
which
   Lie tumbling in my barefoot way, and mount
   Their pricks at my footfall; sometime am I
   All wound with adders, who with cloven
tongues
   Do hiss me into madness.

Enter TRINCULO

   Lo, now, lo!
   Here comes a spirit of his, and to torment me
   For bringing wood in slowly. I'll fall flat;
   Perchance he will not mind me.
  TRINCULO. Here's neither bush nor shrub to
bear off any weather at all, and another storm
brewing; I hear it sing i' th' wind. Yond same
black cloud, yond huge one, looks like a foul

bombard that would shed his liquor. If it should thunder as it did before, I know not where to hide my head. Yond same cloud cannot choose but fall by pailfuls. What have we here? a man or a fish? dead or alive? A fish: he smells like a fish; a very ancient and fish-like smell; kind of not-of-the-newest Poor-John. A strange fish! Were I in England now, as once I was, and had but this fish painted, not a holiday fool there but would give a piece of silver. There would this monster make a man; any strange beast there makes a man; when they will not give a doit to relieve a lame beggar, they will lay out ten to see a dead Indian. Legg'd like a man, and his fins like arms! Warm, o' my troth! I do now let loose my opinion; hold it no longer: this is no fish, but an islander, that hath lately suffered by thunderbolt. [Thunder] Alas, the storm is come again! My best way is to creep under his gaberdine; there is no other shelter hereabout. Misery acquaints a man with strange bedfellows. I will here shroud till the dregs of the storm be past.

Enter STEPHANO singing; a bottle in his hand

STEPHANO. I shall no more to sea, to sea,
   Here shall I die ashore-
   This is a very scurvy tune to sing at a man's funeral; well, here's my comfort.
          [Drinks]

The master, the swabber, the boatswain, and I,
   The gunner, and his mate,
   Lov'd Mall, Meg, and Marian, and Margery,
   But none of us car'd for Kate;
   For she had a tongue with a tang,

Would cry to a sailor 'Go hang!'

She lov'd not the savour of tar nor of pitch,

Yet a tailor might scratch her where'er she did itch.

Then to sea, boys, and let her go hang!

This is a scurvy tune too; but here's my comfort.

[Drinks]

CALIBAN. Do not torment me. O!

STEPHANO. What's the matter? Have we devils here? Do you put tricks upon 's with savages and men of Ind? Ha! I have not scap'd drowning to be afeard now of your four legs; for it hath been said: As proper a man as ever went on four legs cannot make him give ground; and is shall be said so again, while Stephano breathes at nostrils.

CALIBAN. The spirit torments me. O!

STEPHANO. This is some monster of the isle with four legs, who hath got, as I take it, an ague. Where the devil should he learn our language? I will give him some relief, if it be but for that. If I can recover him, and keep him tame, and get to Naples with him, he's a present for any emperor that ever trod on neat's leather.

CALIBAN. Do not torment me, prithee; I'll bring my wood home faster.

STEPHANO. He's in his fit now, and does not talk after the wisest. He shall taste of my bottle; if he have never drunk wine afore, it will go near to remove his fit. If I can recover him, and keep him tame, I will not take too much for him; he shall pay for him that hath him, and that soundly.

CALIBAN. Thou dost me yet but little hurt; thou wilt anon,

I know it by thy trembling; now Prosper works upon thee.

STEPHANO. Come on your ways; open your mouth; here is that which will give language to you, cat. Open your mouth; this will shake your shaking, I can tell you, and that soundly; you cannot tell who's your friend. Open your chaps again.

TRINCULO. I should know that voice; it should be-but he is

drown'd; and these are devils. O, defend me!

STEPHANO. Four legs and two voices; a most delicate monster! His forward voice, now, is to speak well of his friend; his backward voice is to utter foul speeches and to detract. If all the wine in my bottle will recover him, I will help his ague. Come-Amen! I will pour some in thy other mouth.

TRINCULO. Stephano!

STEPHANO. Doth thy other mouth call me? Mercy, mercy! This is a devil, and no monster; I will leave him; I have no long spoon.

TRINCULO. Stephano! If thou beest Stephano, touch me, and speak to me; for I am Trinculo- be not afeard-thy good friend Trinculo.

STEPHANO. If thou beest Trinculo, come forth; I'll pull the by the lesser legs; if any be Trinculo's legs, these are they. Thou art very Trinculo indeed! How cam'st thou to be the siege of this moon-calf? Can he vent Trinculos?

TRINCULO. I took him to be kill'd with a thunderstroke. But art thou not drown'd, Stephano? I hope now thou are not drown'd. Is the storm overblown? I hid me under the dead moon-calf's gaberdine for fear of the storm. And art thou living, Stephano? O Stephano, two Neapolitans scap'd!

STEPHANO. Prithee, do not turn me about; my stomach is not constant.

CALIBAN. [Aside] These be fine things, an if they be not sprites.

That's a brave god, and bears celestial liquor.

I will kneel to him.

STEPHANO. How didst thou scape? How cam'st thou hither?

Swear by this bottle how thou cam'st hither- I escap'd upon a butt of sack, which the sailors heaved o'erboard- by this bottle, which I made of the bark of a tree, with mine own hands, since I was cast ashore.

CALIBAN. I'll swear upon that bottle to be thy true subject, for the liquor is not earthly.

STEPHANO. Here; swear then how thou escap'dst.

TRINCULO. Swum ashore, man, like a duck; I can swim like a duck, I'll be sworn.

STEPHANO. [Passing the bottle] Here, kiss the book. Though thou canst swim like a duck, thou art made like a goose.

TRINCULO. O Stephano, hast any more of this?

STEPHANO. The whole butt, man; my cellar is in a rock by

th' seaside, where my wine is hid. How now, moon-calf!

How does thine ague?

CALIBAN. Hast thou not dropp'd from heaven?

STEPHANO. Out o' th' moon, I do assure thee; I was the Man

i' th' Moon, when time was.

CALIBAN. I have seen thee in her, and I do adore thee. My mistress show'd me thee, and thy dog and thy bush.

STEPHANO. Come, swear to that; kiss the book. I will furnish it anon with new contents. Swear.

[CALIBAN drinks]

TRINCULO. By this good light, this is a very shallow monster!

I afeard of him! A very weak monster! The Man i' th'

Moon! A most poor credulous monster! Well drawn, monster, in good sooth!

CALIBAN. I'll show thee every fertile inch o' th' island; and will kiss thy foot. I prithee be my god.

TRINCULO. By this light, a most perfidious and drunken monster! When's god's asleep he'll rob his bottle.

CALIBAN. I'll kiss thy foot; I'll swear myself thy subject.

STEPHANO. Come on, then; down, and swear.

TRINCULO. I shall laugh myself to death at this puppy- headed monster. A most scurvy monster! I could find in my heart to beat him-

STEPHANO. Come, kiss.

TRINCULO. But that the poor monster's in drink. An abominable monster!

CALIBAN. I'll show thee the best springs; I'll pluck thee berries;

I'll fish for thee, and get thee wood enough.

A plague upon the tyrant that I serve!

I'll bear him no more sticks, but follow thee,

Thou wondrous man.

TRINCULO. A most ridiculous monster, to make a wonder of a poor drunkard!

CALIBAN. I prithee let me bring thee where crabs grow;

And I with my long nails will dig thee pig-nuts;

Show thee a jay's nest, and instruct thee how

To snare the nimble marmoset; I'll bring thee

To clust'ring filberts, and sometimes I'll get thee

Young scamels from the rock. Wilt thou go with me?

STEPHANO. I prithee now, lead the way without any more talking. Trinculo, the King and all our company else being drown'd, we will inherit here. Here, bear my bottle.

Fellow Trinculo, we'll fill him by and by again.

CALIBAN. [Sings drunkenly] Farewell, master; farewell, farewell!

TRINCULO. A howling monster; a drunken monster!

CALIBAN. No more dams I'll make for fish;
  Nor fetch in firing
  At requiring,
  Nor scrape trenchering, nor wash dish.

'Ban 'Ban, Ca-Caliban,

Has a new master-Get a new man.

Freedom, high-day! high-day, freedom!

freedom, high- day, freedom!

STEPHANO. O brave monster! Lead the way.

Exeunt

ACT III. SCENE 1

Before PROSPERO'S cell

Enter FERDINAND, hearing a log

FERDINAND. There be some sports are painful, and their

  labour

  Delight in them sets off; some kinds of baseness

  Are nobly undergone, and most poor matters

  Point to rich ends. This my mean task

  Would be as heavy to me as odious, but

  The mistress which I serve quickens what's dead,

  And makes my labours pleasures. O, she is

Ten times more gentle than her father's
crabbed;
And he's compos'd of harshness. I must
remove
Some thousands of these logs, and pile them
up,
Upon a sore injunction; my sweet mistress
Weeps when she sees me work, and says
such baseness
Had never like executor. I forget;
But these sweet thoughts do even refresh
my labours,
Most busy, least when I do it.

Enter MIRANDA; and PROSPERO at a
distance, unseen

MIRANDA. Alas, now; pray you,
Work not so hard; I would the lightning had

Burnt up those logs that you are enjoin'd to pile.

Pray, set it down and rest you; when this burns,

'Twill weep for having wearied you. My father

Is hard at study; pray, now, rest yourself;

He's safe for these three hours.

FERDINAND. O most dear mistress,

The sun will set before I shall discharge

What I must strive to do.

MIRANDA. If you'll sit down,

I'll bear your logs the while; pray give me that;

I'll carry it to the pile.

FERDINAND. No, precious creature;

I had rather crack my sinews, break my back,

Than you should such dishonour undergo,

While I sit lazy by.

MIRANDA. It would become me

As well as it does you; and I should do it

With much more ease; for my good will is to it,

And yours it is against.

PROSPERO. [Aside] Poor worm, thou art infected!

This visitation shows it.

MIRANDA. You look wearily.

FERDINAND. No, noble mistress; 'tis fresh morning with me

When you are by at night. I do beseech you,

Chiefly that I might set it in my prayers,

What is your name?

MIRANDA. Miranda-O my father,

I have broke your hest to say so!

FERDINAND. Admir'd Miranda!

What's dearest to the world! Full many a lady

I have ey'd with best regard; and many a
time
Th' harmony of their tongues hath into
bondage
Brought my too diligent ear; for several
virtues
Have I lik'd several women, never any
With so full soul, but some defect in her
Did quarrel with the noblest grace she ow'd,
And put it to the foil; but you, O you,
So perfect and so peerless, are created
Of every creature's best!
MIRANDA. I do not know
One of my sex; no woman's face remember,
Save, from my glass, mine own; nor have I
seen
More that I may call men than you, good
friend,
And my dear father. How features are
abroad,

I am skilless of; but, by my modesty,

The jewel in my dower, I would not wish

Any companion in the world but you;

Nor can imagination form a shape,

Besides yourself, to like of. But I prattle

Something too wildly, and my father's precepts

I therein do forget.

FERDINAND. I am, in my condition,

A prince, Miranda; I do think, a king-

I would not so!-and would no more endure

This wooden slavery than to suffer

The flesh-fly blow my mouth. Hear my soul speak:

The very instant that I saw you, did

My heart fly to your service; there resides

To make me slave to it; and for your sake

Am I this patient log-man.

MIRANDA. Do you love me?

FERDINAND. O heaven, O earth, bear witness
to this sound,

And crown what I profess with kind event,

If I speak true! If hollowly, invert

What best is boded me to mischief! I,

Beyond all limit of what else i' th' world,

Do love, prize, honour you.

MIRANDA. I am a fool

To weep at what I am glad of.

PROSPERO. [Aside] Fair encounter

Of two most rare affections! Heavens rain
grace

On that which breeds between 'em!

FERDINAND. Wherefore weep you?

MIRANDA. At mine unworthiness, that dare
not offer

What I desire to give, and much less take

What I shall die to want. But this is trifling;

And all the more it seeks to hide itself,

The bigger bulk it shows. Hence, bashful cunning!

And prompt me, plain and holy innocence!

I am your wife, if you will marry me;

If not, I'll die your maid. To be your fellow

You may deny me; but I'll be your servant,

Whether you will or no.

FERDINAND. My mistress, dearest;

And I thus humble ever.

MIRANDA. My husband, then?

FERDINAND. Ay, with a heart as willing

As bondage e'er of freedom. Here's my hand.

MIRANDA. And mine, with my heart in't. And now farewell

Till half an hour hence.

FERDINAND. A thousand thousand!

Exeunt FERDINAND and MIRANDA severally

PROSPERO. So glad of this as they I cannot be,

Who are surpris'd withal; but my rejoicing

At nothing can be more. I'll to my book;

For yet ere supper time must I perform

Much business appertaining.

Exit

SCENE 2

Another part of the island

Enter CALIBAN, STEPHANO, and TRINCULO

STEPHANO. Tell not me-when the butt is out
we will drink water, not a drop before;
therefore bear up, and board 'em. Servant-
monster, drink to me.

TRINCULO. Servant-monster! The folly of this
island! They say there's but five upon this isle:
we are three of them; if th' other two be
brain'd like us, the state totters.

STEPHANO. Drink, servant-monster, when I
bid thee; thy eyes are almost set in thy head.

TRINCULO. Where should they be set else? He
were a brave monster indeed, if they were set
in his tail.

STEPHANO. My man-monster hath drown'd his tongue in sack. For my part, the sea cannot drown me; I swam, ere I could recover the shore, five and thirty leagues, off and on. By this light, thou shalt be my lieutenant, monster, or my standard.

TRINCULO. Your lieutenant, if you list; he's no standard.

STEPHANO. We'll not run, Monsieur Monster.

TRINCULO. Nor go neither; but you'll lie like dogs, and yet say nothing neither.

STEPHANO. Moon-calf, speak once in thy life, if thou beest a good moon-calf.

CALIBAN. How does thy honour? Let me lick thy shoe.

I'll not serve him; he is not valiant.

TRINCULO. Thou liest, most ignorant monster: I am in case to justle a constable. Why, thou debosh'd fish, thou, was there ever man a coward that hath drunk so much sack as

I to-day? Wilt thou tell a monstrous lie, being but half fish and half a monster?

CALIBAN. Lo, how he mocks me! Wilt thou let him, my lord?

TRINCULO. 'Lord' quoth he! That a monster should be such a natural!

CALIBAN. Lo, lo again! Bite him to death, I prithee.

STEPHANO. Trinculo, keep a good tongue in your head; if you prove a mutineer-the next tree! The poor monster's my subject, and he shall not suffer indignity.

CALIBAN. I thank my noble lord. Wilt thou be pleas'd to hearken once again to the suit I made to thee?

STEPHANO. Marry will I; kneel and repeat it; I will stand, and so shall Trinculo.

Enter ARIEL, invisible

CALIBAN. As I told thee before, I am subject to a tyrant, sorcerer, that by his cunning hath cheated me of the island.

ARIEL. Thou liest.

CALIBAN. Thou liest, thou jesting monkey, thou; I would my valiant master would destroy thee. I do not lie.

STEPHANO. Trinculo, if you trouble him any more in's tale, by this hand, I will supplant some of your teeth.

TRINCULO. Why, I said nothing.

STEPHANO. Mum, then, and no more. Proceed.

CALIBAN. I say, by sorcery he got this isle;
From me he got it. If thy greatness will
Revenge it on him-for I know thou dar'st,
But this thing dare not-

STEPHANO. That's most certain.

CALIBAN. Thou shalt be lord of it, and I'll serve thee.

STEPHANO. How now shall this be compass'd? Canst thou bring me to the party?

CALIBAN. Yea, yea, my lord; I'll yield him thee asleep,

Where thou mayst knock a nail into his head.

ARIEL. Thou liest; thou canst not.

CALIBAN. What a pied ninny's this! Thou scurvy patch!

I do beseech thy greatness, give him blows,

And take his bottle from him. When that's gone

He shall drink nought but brine; for I'll not show him

Where the quick freshes are.

STEPHANO. Trinculo, run into no further danger; interrupt the monster one word further and, by this hand, I'll turn my mercy out o' doors, and make a stock-fish of thee.

TRINCULO. Why, what did I? I did nothing. I'll go farther off.

STEPHANO. Didst thou not say he lied?

ARIEL. Thou liest.

STEPHANO. Do I so? Take thou that. [Beats him] As you like this, give me the lie another time.

TRINCULO. I did not give the lie. Out o' your wits and hearing too? A pox o' your bottle! This can sack and drinking do. A murrain on your monster, and the devil take your fingers!

CALIBAN. Ha, ha, ha!

STEPHANO. Now, forward with your tale.- Prithee stand further off.

CALIBAN. Beat him enough; after a little time, I'll beat him too.

STEPHANO. Stand farther. Come, proceed.

CALIBAN. Why, as I told thee, 'tis a custom with him I' th' afternoon to sleep; there thou mayst brain him,

Having first seiz'd his books; or with a log

Batter his skull, or paunch him with a stake,

Or cut his wezand with thy knife. Remember

First to possess his books; for without them

He's but a sot, as I am, nor hath not

One spirit to command; they all do hate him

As rootedly as I. Burn but his books.

He has brave utensils-for so he calls them-

Which, when he has a house, he'll deck

withal.

And that most deeply to consider is

The beauty of his daughter; he himself

Calls her a nonpareil. I never saw a woman

But only Sycorax my dam and she;

But she as far surpasseth Sycorax

As great'st does least.

STEPHANO. Is it so brave a lass?

CALIBAN. Ay, lord; she will become thy bed, I

warrant,

And bring thee forth brave brood.

STEPHANO. Monster, I will kill this man; his

daughter and I will be King and Queen-save

our Graces!-and Trinculo and thyself shall be viceroys. Dost thou like the plot,

   Trinculo?

TRINCULO. Excellent.

STEPHANO. Give me thy hand; I am sorry I beat thee; but while thou liv'st, keep a good tongue in thy head.

CALIBAN. Within this half hour will he be asleep.

   Wilt thou destroy him then?

STEPHANO. Ay, on mine honour.

ARIEL. This will I tell my master.

CALIBAN. Thou mak'st me merry; I am full of pleasure.

   Let us be jocund; will you troll the catch

   You taught me but while-ere?

STEPHANO. At thy request, monster, I will do reason, any reason. Come on, Trinculo, let us sing.

   [Sings]

Flout 'em and scout 'em,

And scout 'em and flout 'em;

Thought is free.

CALIBAN. That's not the tune.

[ARIEL plays the tune on a tabor
and pipe]

STEPHANO. What is this same?

TRINCULO. This is the tune of our catch,
play'd by the picture of Nobody.

STEPHANO. If thou beest a man, show thyself
in thy likeness; if thou beest a devil, take't as
thou list.

TRINCULO. O, forgive me my sins!

STEPHANO. He that dies pays all debts. I defy
thee. Mercy upon us!

CALIBAN. Art thou afeard?

STEPHANO. No, monster, not I.

CALIBAN. Be not afeard. The isle is full of noises,

Sounds, and sweet airs, that give delight, and hurt not.

Sometimes a thousand twangling instruments

Will hum about mine ears; and sometimes voices,

That, if I then had wak'd after long sleep,

Will make me sleep again; and then, in dreaming,

The clouds methought would open and show riches

Ready to drop upon me, that, when I wak'd,

I cried to dream again.

STEPHANO. This will prove a brave kingdom to me, where I shall have my music for nothing.

CALIBAN. When Prospero is destroy'd.

STEPHANO. That shall be by and by; I remember the story.

TRINCULO. The sound is going away; let's follow it, and after do our work.

STEPHANO. Lead, monster; we'll follow. I would I could see this taborer; he lays it on.

TRINCULO. Wilt come? I'll follow, Stephano.

Exeunt

SCENE 3

Another part of the island

Enter ALONSO, SEBASTIAN, ANTONIO,
GONZALO, ADRIAN, FRANCISCO, and
OTHERS

GONZALO. By'r lakin, I can go no further, sir;
  My old bones ache. Here's a maze trod,
indeed,
  Through forth-rights and meanders! By your
patience,
  I needs must rest me.
 ALONSO. Old lord, I cannot blame thee,
  Who am myself attach'd with weariness
  To th' dulling of my spirits; sit down and
rest.
  Even here I will put off my hope, and keep it

No longer for my flatterer; he is drown'd

Whom thus we stray to find, and the sea
mocks

Our frustrate search on land. Well, let him
go.

  ANTONIO. [Aside to SEBASTIAN] I am right
glad that he's so out of hope.

Do not, for one repulse, forgo the purpose

That you resolv'd t' effect.

  SEBASTIAN. [Aside to ANTONIO] The next
advantage

Will we take throughly.

  ANTONIO. [Aside to SEBASTIAN] Let it be to-
night;

For, now they are oppress'd with travel, they

Will not, nor cannot, use such vigilance

As when they are fresh.

  SEBASTIAN. [Aside to ANTONIO] I say, to-
night; no more.

*Solemn and strange music; and
PROSPERO on the top, invisible. Enter several
strange SHAPES, bringing in a banquet; and
dance about it with gentle actions of
salutations; and inviting the KING, etc., to eat,
they depart*

ALONSO. What harmony is this? My good
friends, hark!

GONZALO. Marvellous sweet music!

ALONSO. Give us kind keepers, heavens!
What were these?

SEBASTIAN. A living drollery. Now I will
believe

That there are unicorns; that in Arabia

There is one tree, the phoenix' throne, one
phoenix

At this hour reigning-there.

ANTONIO. I'll believe both;

And what does else want credit, come to me,

And I'll be sworn 'tis true; travellers ne'er
did lie,

Though fools at home condemn 'em.

GONZALO. If in Naples

I should report this now, would they believe
me?

If I should say, I saw such islanders,

For certes these are people of the island,

Who though they are of monstrous shape
yet, note,

Their manners are more gentle-kind than of

Our human generation you shall find

Many, nay, almost any.

PROSPERO. [Aside] Honest lord,

Thou hast said well; for some of you there
present

Are worse than devils.

ALONSO. I cannot too much muse

Such shapes, such gesture, and such sound,
expressing,

Although they want the use of tongue, a kind

Of excellent dumb discourse.

PROSPERO. [Aside] Praise in departing.

FRANCISCO. They vanish'd strangely.

SEBASTIAN. No matter, since

They have left their viands behind; for we
have stomachs.

Will't please you taste of what is here?

ALONSO. Not I.

GONZALO. Faith, sir, you need not fear. When
we were boys,

Who would believe that there were
mountaineers,

Dewlapp'd like bulls, whose throats had
hanging at 'em

Wallets of flesh? or that there were such
men

Whose heads stood in their breasts? which
now we find

Each putter-out of five for one will bring us

Good warrant of.

ALONSO. I will stand to, and feed,

Although my last; no matter, since I feel

The best is past. Brother, my lord the Duke,

Stand to, and do as we.

Thunder and lightning. Enter ARIEL, like a harpy; claps his wings upon the table; and, with a quaint device, the banquet vanishes

ARIEL. You are three men of sin, whom Destiny,

That hath to instrument this lower world

And what is in't, the never-surfeited sea

Hath caus'd to belch up you; and on this island

Where man doth not inhabit-you 'mongst men

Being most unfit to live. I have made you mad;

And even with such-like valour men hang and drown

Their proper selves.

[*ALONSO, SEBASTIAN etc., draw their swords*]

You fools! I and my fellows

Are ministers of Fate; the elements

Of whom your swords are temper'd may as well

Wound the loud winds, or with bemock'd-at stabs

Kill the still-closing waters, as diminish

One dowle that's in my plume; my fellow-ministers

Are like invulnerable. If you could hurt,

Your swords are now too massy for your strengths

And will not be uplifted. But remember-

For that's my business to you-that you three

From Milan did supplant good Prospero;

Expos'd unto the sea, which hath requit it,

Him, and his innocent child; for which foul
deed

The pow'rs, delaying, not forgetting, have

Incens'd the seas and shores, yea, all the
creatures,

Against your peace. Thee of thy son, Alonso,

They have bereft; and do pronounce by me

Ling'ring perdition, worse than any death

Can be at once, shall step by step attend

You and your ways; whose wraths to guard
you from-

Which here, in this most desolate isle, else
falls

Upon your heads-is nothing but heart's
sorrow,

And a clear life ensuing.

He vanishes in thunder; then, to soft music, enter the SHAPES again, and dance, with mocks and mows, and carrying out the table

PROSPERO. Bravely the figure of this harpy hast thou

Perform'd, my Ariel; a grace it had, devouring.

Of my instruction hast thou nothing bated

In what thou hadst to say; so, with good life

And observation strange, my meaner ministers

Their several kinds have done. My high charms work,

And these mine enemies are all knit up

In their distractions. They now are in my pow'r;

And in these fits I leave them, while I visit

Young Ferdinand, whom they suppose is drown'd,

And his and mine lov'd darling.   Exit
above

  GONZALO. I' th' name of something holy, sir,
why stand you

   In this strange stare?

  ALONSO. O, it is monstrous, monstrous!

   Methought the billows spoke, and told me of
it;

   The winds did sing it to me; and the thunder,

   That deep and dreadful organ-pipe,
pronounc'd

   The name of Prosper; it did bass my
trespass.

   Therefore my son i' th' ooze is bedded; and

   I'll seek him deeper than e'er plummet
sounded,

   And with him there lie mudded.

                        Exit

  SEBASTIAN. But one fiend at a time,

   I'll fight their legions o'er.

ANTONIO. I'll be thy second.

Exeunt SEBASTIAN and ANTONIO

GONZALO. All three of them are desperate;
their great guilt,

Like poison given to work a great time after,

Now gins to bite the spirits. I do beseech
you,

That are of suppler joints, follow them
swiftly,

And hinder them from what this ecstasy

May now provoke them to.

ADRIAN. Follow, I pray you.

Exeunt

ACT IV. SCENE 1

Before PROSPERO'S cell

Enter PROSPERO, FERDINAND, and MIRANDA

  PROSPERO. If I have too austerely punish'd you,
    Your compensation makes amends; for
    Have given you here a third of mine own life,
    Or that for which I live; who once again
    I tender to thy hand. All thy vexations
    Were but my trials of thy love, and thou
    Hast strangely stood the test; here, afore heaven,
    I ratify this my rich gift. O Ferdinand!
    Do not smile at me that I boast her off,
    For thou shalt find she will outstrip all praise,

And make it halt behind her.

FERDINAND. I do believe it

Against an oracle.

PROSPERO. Then, as my gift, and thine own
acquisition

Wort'hily purchas'd, take my daughter. But

If thou dost break her virgin-knot before

All sanctimonious ceremonies may

With full and holy rite be minist'red,

No sweet aspersion shall the heavens let fall

To make this contract grow; but barren hate,

Sour-ey'd disdain, and discord, shall bestrew

The union of your bed with weeds so loathly

That you shall hate it both. Therefore take
heed,

As Hymen's lamps shall light you.

FERDINAND. As I hope

For quiet days, fair issue, and long life,

With such love as 'tis now, the murkiest den,

The most opportune place, the strong'st suggestion

Our worser genius can, shall never melt

Mine honour into lust, to take away

The edge of that day's celebration,

When I shall think or Phoebus' steeds are founder'd

Or Night kept chain'd below.

PROSPERO. Fairly spoke.

Sit, then, and talk with her; she is thine own.

What, Ariel! my industrious servant, Ariel!

Enter ARIEL

ARIEL. What would my potent master? Here I am.

PROSPERO. Thou and thy meaner fellows your last service

Did worthily perform; and I must use you

In such another trick. Go bring the rabble,

O'er whom I give thee pow'r, here to this
place.

    Incite them to quick motion; for I must

    Bestow upon the eyes of this young couple

    Some vanity of mine art; it is my promise,

    And they expect it from me.

ARIEL. Presently?

PROSPERO. Ay, with a twink.

ARIEL. Before you can say 'come' and 'go,'

    And breathe twice, and cry 'so, so,'

    Each one, tripping on his toe,

    Will be here with mop and mow.

    Do you love me, master? No?

PROSPERO. Dearly, my delicate Ariel. Do not
approach

    Till thou dost hear me call.

ARIEL. Well! I conceive.

Exit

PROSPERO. Look thou be true; do not give
dalliance

Too much the rein; the strongest oaths are straw

To th' fire i' th' blood. Be more abstemious,

Or else good night your vow!

FERDINAND. I warrant you, sir,

The white cold virgin snow upon my heart

Abates the ardour of my liver.

PROSPERO. Well!

Now come, my Ariel, bring a corollary,

Rather than want a spirit; appear, and pertly.

No tongue! All eyes! Be silent.

[Soft music]

Enter IRIS

IRIS. Ceres, most bounteous lady, thy rich leas

Of wheat, rye, barley, vetches, oats, and pease;

Thy turfy mountains, where live nibbling sheep,

And flat meads thatch'd with stover, them to
keep;

   Thy banks with pioned and twilled brims,

   Which spongy April at thy hest betrims,

   To make cold nymphs chaste crowns; and
thy broom groves,

   Whose shadow the dismissed bachelor loves,

   Being lass-lorn; thy pole-clipt vineyard;

   And thy sea-marge, sterile and rocky hard,

   Where thou thyself dost air-the Queen o' th'
sky,

   Whose wat'ry arch and messenger am I,

   Bids thee leave these; and with her
sovereign grace,

   Here on this grass-plot, in this very place,

   To come and sport. Her peacocks fly amain.

                    [JUNO descends in her car]

Approach, rich Ceres, her to entertain.

                    Enter CERES

CERES. Hail, many-coloured messenger, that ne'er

   Dost disobey the wife of Jupiter;

   Who, with thy saffron wings, upon my flow'rs

   Diffusest honey drops, refreshing show'rs;

   And with each end of thy blue bow dost crown

   My bosky acres and my unshrubb'd down,

   Rich scarf to my proud earth-why hath thy Queen

   Summon'd me hither to this short-grass'd green?

  IRIS. A contract of true love to celebrate,

   And some donation freely to estate

   On the blest lovers.

  CERES. Tell me, heavenly bow,

   If Venus or her son, as thou dost know,

Do now attend the Queen? Since they did
plot

    The means that dusky Dis my daughter got,

    Her and her blind boy's scandal'd company

    I have forsworn.

 IRIS. Of her society

    Be not afraid. I met her Deity

    Cutting the clouds towards Paphos, and her
son

    Dove-drawn with her. Here thought they to
have done

    Some wanton charm upon this man and
maid,

    Whose vows are that no bed-rite shall be
paid

    Till Hymen's torch be lighted; but in vain.

    Mars's hot minion is return'd again;

    Her waspish-headed son has broke his
arrows,

Swears he will shoot no more, but play with
sparrows,

   And be a boy right out.

       [JUNO alights]

 CERES. Highest Queen of State,

   Great Juno, comes; I know her by her gait.

   JUNO. How does my bounteous sister? Go
with me

   To bless this twain, that they may
prosperous be,

   And honour'd in their issue.

       [They sing]

 JUNO. Honour, riches, marriage-blessing,

   Long continuance, and increasing,

   Hourly joys be still upon you!

   Juno sings her blessings on you.

 CERES. Earth's increase, foison plenty,

   Barns and gamers never empty;

   Vines with clust'ring bunches growing,

   Plants with goodly burden bowing;

Spring come to you at the farthest,

In the very end of harvest!

Scarcity and want shall shun you,

Ceres' blessing so is on you.

FERDINAND. This is a most majestic vision,
and

Harmonious charmingly. May I be bold

To think these spirits?

PROSPERO. Spirits, which by mine art

I have from their confines call'd to enact

My present fancies.

FERDINAND. Let me live here ever;

So rare a wond'red father and a wise

Makes this place Paradise.

*[JUNO and CERES whisper, and send IRIS
on employment]*

PROSPERO. Sweet now, silence;

Juno and Ceres whisper seriously.

There's something else to do; hush, and be
mute,

Or else our spell is marr'd.

IRIS. You nymphs, call'd Naiads, of the wind'ring brooks,

With your sedg'd crowns and ever harmless looks,

Leave your crisp channels, and on this green land

Answer your summons; Juno does command.

Come, temperate nymphs, and help to celebrate

A contract of true love; be not too late.

Enter certain NYMPHS

You sun-burnt sicklemen, of August weary,

Come hither from the furrow, and be merry;

Make holiday; your rye-straw hats put on,

And these fresh nymphs encounter every one in country footing.

Enter certain REAPERS, properly habited; they join with the NYMPHS in a graceful dance; towards the end whereof PROSPERO starts suddenly, and speaks, after which, to a strange, hollow, and confused noise, they heavily vanish

PROSPERO. [Aside] I had forgot that foul conspiracy
   Of the beast Caliban and his confederates
   Against my life; the minute of their plot
   Is almost come. [To the SPIRITS] Well done; avoid; no more!
   FERDINAND. This is strange; your father's in some passion
   That works him strongly.
   MIRANDA. Never till this day
   Saw I him touch'd with anger so distemper'd.

PROSPERO. You do look, my son, in a mov'd sort,

As if you were dismay'd; be cheerful, sir.

Our revels now are ended. These our actors,

As I foretold you, were all spirits, and

Are melted into air, into thin air;

And, like the baseless fabric of this vision,

The cloud-capp'd towers, the gorgeous palaces,

The solemn temples, the great globe itself,

Yea, all which it inherit, shall dissolve,

And, like this insubstantial pageant faded,

Leave not a rack behind. We are such stuff

As dreams are made on; and our little life

Is rounded with a sleep. Sir, I am vex'd;

Bear with my weakness; my old brain is troubled;

Be not disturb'd with my infirmity.

If you be pleas'd, retire into my cell

And there repose; a turn or two I'll walk

To still my beating mind.

FERDINAND, MIRANDA. We wish your peace.

Exeunt

PROSPERO. Come, with a thought. I thank thee, Ariel; come.

Enter ARIEL

ARIEL. Thy thoughts I cleave to. What's thy pleasure?

PROSPERO. Spirit,

We must prepare to meet with Caliban.

ARIEL. Ay, my commander. When I presented 'Ceres.'

I thought to have told thee of it; but I fear'd

Lest I might anger thee.

PROSPERO. Say again, where didst thou leave these varlets?

ARIEL. I told you, sir, they were red-hot with drinking;

So full of valour that they smote the air

For breathing in their faces; beat the ground

For kissing of their feet; yet always bending

Towards their project. Then I beat my tabor,

At which like unback'd colts they prick'd
their ears,

Advanc'd their eyelids, lifted up their noses

As they smelt music; so I charm'd their ears,

That calf-like they my lowing follow'd
through

Tooth'd briers, sharp furzes, pricking goss,
and thorns,

Which ent'red their frail shins. At last I left
them

I' th' filthy mantled pool beyond your cell,

There dancing up to th' chins, that the foul
lake

O'erstunk their feet.

PROSPERO. This was well done, my bird.

Thy shape invisible retain thou still.

The trumpery in my house, go bring it hither

For stale to catch these thieves.

ARIEL. I go, I go.   Exit

PROSPERO. A devil, a born devil, on whose nature

Nurture can never stick; on whom my pains,

Humanely taken, all, all lost, quite lost;

And as with age his body uglier grows,

So his mind cankers. I will plague them all,

Even to roaring.

Re-enter ARIEL, loaden with glistering apparel, &c.

Come, hang them on this line.

[PROSPERO and ARIEL remain, invisible]

Enter CALIBAN, STEPHANO, and TRINCULO, all wet

CALIBAN. Pray you, tread softly, that the blind mole may not

  Hear a foot fall; we now are near his cell.

  STEPHANO. Monster, your fairy, which you say is a harmless fairy, has done little better than play'd the Jack with us.

  TRINCULO. Monster, I do smell all horse-piss at which my nose is in great indignation.

  STEPHANO. So is mine. Do you hear, monster? If I should take a displeasure against you, look you-

  TRINCULO. Thou wert but a lost monster.

  CALIBAN. Good my lord, give me thy favour still.

  Be patient, for the prize I'll bring thee to

  Shall hoodwink this mischance; therefore speak softly.

  All's hush'd as midnight yet.

  TRINCULO. Ay, but to lose our bottles in the pool!

STEPHANO. There is not only disgrace and dishonour in that, monster, but an infinite loss.

TRINCULO. That's more to me than my wetting; yet this is your harmless fairy, monster.

STEPHANO. I will fetch off my bottle, though I be o'er ears for my labour.

CALIBAN. Prithee, my king, be quiet. Seest thou here,

This is the mouth o' th' cell; no noise, and enter.

Do that good mischief which may make this island

Thine own for ever, and I, thy Caliban,

For aye thy foot-licker.

STEPHANO. Give me thy hand. I do begin to have bloody thoughts.

TRINCULO. O King Stephano! O peer! O worthy Stephano!

Look what a wardrobe here is for thee!

CALIBAN. Let it alone, thou fool; it is but trash.

TRINCULO. O, ho, monster; we know what belongs to a frippery. O King Stephano!

STEPHANO. Put off that gown, Trinculo; by this hand, I'll have that gown.

TRINCULO. Thy Grace shall have it.

CALIBAN. The dropsy drown this fool! What do you mean
　To dote thus on such luggage? Let 't alone,
　And do the murder first. If he awake,
　From toe to crown he'll fill our skins with pinches;
　Make us strange stuff.

STEPHANO. Be you quiet, monster. Mistress line, is not this my jerkin? Now is the jerkin under the line; now, jerkin, you are like to lose your hair, and prove a bald jerkin.

TRINCULO. Do, do. We steal by line and level, an't like your Grace.

STEPHANO. I thank thee for that jest; here's a garment for't. Wit shall not go unrewarded while I am king of this country. 'Steal by line and level' is an excellent pass of pate; there's another garmet for't.

TRINCULO. Monster, come, put some lime upon your fingers, and away with the rest.

CALIBAN. I will have none on't. We shall lose our time,

And all be turn'd to barnacles, or to apes
With foreheads villainous low.

STEPHANO. Monster, lay-to your fingers; help to bear this away where my hogshead of wine is, or I'll turn you out of my kingdom. Go to, carry this.

TRINCULO. And this.

STEPHANO. Ay, and this.

A noise of hunters beard. Enter divers SPIRITS,
in shape of dogs and hounds, bunting them
about; PROSPERO and ARIEL setting them on

PROSPERO. Hey, Mountain, hey!

ARIEL. Silver! there it goes, Silver!

PROSPERO. Fury, Fury! There, Tyrant, there!
Hark, hark!

      [CALIBAN, STEPHANO, and TRINCULO
are driven out]

Go charge my goblins that they grind their
joints

With dry convulsions, shorten up their
sinews

With aged cramps, and more pinch-spotted
make them

Than pard or cat o' mountain.

ARIEL. Hark, they roar.

PROSPERO. Let them be hunted soundly. At
this hour

Lies at my mercy all mine enemies.

Shortly shall all my labours end, and thou

Shalt have the air at freedom; for a little

Follow, and do me service.

Exeunt

ACT V. SCENE 1

Before PROSPERO'S cell

Enter PROSPERO in his magic robes, and ARIEL

PROSPERO. Now does my project gather to a head;

My charms crack not, my spirits obey; and time

Goes upright with his carriage. How's the day?

ARIEL. On the sixth hour; at which time, my lord,

You said our work should cease.

PROSPERO. I did say so,

When first I rais'd the tempest. Say, my spirit,

How fares the King and 's followers?

ARIEL. Confin'd together

   In the same fashion as you gave in charge;

   Just as you left them; all prisoners, sir,

   In the line-grove which weather-fends your

cell;

   They cannot budge till your release. The

King,

   His brother, and yours, abide all three

distracted,

   And the remainder mourning over them,

   Brim full of sorrow and dismay; but chiefly

   Him you term'd, sir, 'the good old lord,

Gonzalo';

   His tears run down his beard, like winter's

drops

   From eaves of reeds. Your charm so strongly

works 'em

   That if you now beheld them your affections

   Would become tender.

 PROSPERO. Dost thou think so, spirit?

ARIEL. Mine would, sir, were I human.

PROSPERO. And mine shall.

Hast thou, which art but air, a touch, a
feeling

Of their afflictions, and shall not myself,

One of their kind, that relish all as sharply,

Passion as they, be kindlier mov'd than thou
art?

Though with their high wrongs I am struck
to th' quick,

Yet with my nobler reason 'gainst my fury

Do I take part; the rarer action is

In virtue than in vengeance; they being
penitent,

The sole drift of my purpose doth extend

Not a frown further. Go release them, Ariel;

My charms I'll break, their senses I'll restore,

And they shall be themselves.

ARIEL. I'll fetch them, sir.

Exit

PROSPERO. Ye elves of hills, brooks, standing lakes, and groves;

And ye that on the sands with printless foot

Do chase the ebbing Neptune, and do fly him

When he comes back; you demi-puppets that

By moonshine do the green sour ringlets make,

Whereof the ewe not bites; and you whose pastime

Is to make midnight mushrooms, that rejoice

To hear the solemn curfew; by whose aid-

Weak masters though ye be-I have be-dimm'd

The noontide sun, call'd forth the mutinous winds,

And 'twixt the green sea and the azur'd vault

Set roaring war. To the dread rattling thunder

Have I given fire, and rifted Jove's stout oak

With his own bolt; the strong-bas'd promontory

Have I made shake, and by the spurs pluck'd up

The pine and cedar. Graves at my command

Have wak'd their sleepers, op'd, and let 'em forth,

By my so potent art. But this rough magic

I here abjure; and, when I have requir'd

Some heavenly music-which even now I do-

To work mine end upon their senses that

This airy charm is for, I'll break my staff,

Bury it certain fathoms in the earth,

And deeper than did ever plummet sound

I'll drown my book.

[Solem music]

Here enters ARIEL before; then ALONSO, with

frantic gesture, attended by GONZALO;

SEBASTIAN and ANTONIO in like manner,

attended by ADRIAN and FRANCISCO. They all enter the circle which PROSPERO had made, and there stand charm'd; which PROSPERO observing, speaks

A solemn air, and the best comforter

To an unsettled fancy, cure thy brains,

Now useless, boil'd within thy skull! There stand,

For you are spell-stopp'd.

Holy Gonzalo, honourable man,

Mine eyes, ev'n sociable to the show of thine,

Fall fellowly drops. The charm dissolves apace,

And as the morning steals upon the night,

Melting the darkness, so their rising senses

Begin to chase the ignorant fumes that mantle

Their clearer reason. O good Gonzalo,

My true preserver, and a loyal sir

To him thou follow'st! I will pay thy graces

Home both in word and deed. Most cruelly

Didst thou, Alonso, use me and my daughter;

Thy brother was a furtherer in the act.

Thou art pinch'd for't now, Sebastian. Flesh

and blood,

You, brother mine, that entertain'd ambition,

Expell'd remorse and nature, who, with

Sebastian-

Whose inward pinches therefore are most

strong-

Would here have kill'd your king, I do

forgive thee,

Unnatural though thou art. Their

understanding

Begins to swell, and the approaching tide

Will shortly fill the reasonable shore

That now lies foul and muddy. Not one of

them

That yet looks on me, or would know me. Ariel,

Fetch me the hat and rapier in my cell;

Exit ARIEL

I will discase me, and myself present

As I was sometime Milan. Quickly, spirit

Thou shalt ere long be free.

ARIEL, on returning, sings and helps to attire him

Where the bee sucks, there suck I;

In a cowslip's bell I lie;

There I couch when owls do cry.

On the bat's back I do fly

After summer merrily.

Merrily, merrily shall I live now

Under the blossom that hangs on the bough.

PROSPERO. Why, that's my dainty Ariel! I shall miss thee;

But yet thou shalt have freedom. So, so, so.

To the King's ship, invisible as thou art;

There shalt thou find the mariners asleep

Under the hatches; the master and the boatswain

Being awake, enforce them to this place;

And presently, I prithee.

ARIEL. I drink the air before me, and return

Or ere your pulse twice beat.

Exit

GONZALO. All torment, trouble, wonder and amazement,

Inhabits here. Some heavenly power guide us

Out of this fearful country!

PROSPERO. Behold, Sir King,

The wronged Duke of Milan, Prospero.

For more assurance that a living prince

Does now speak to thee, I embrace thy body;

And to thee and thy company I bid

A hearty welcome.

ALONSO. Whe'er thou be'st he or no,

Or some enchanted trifle to abuse me,

As late I have been, I not know. Thy pulse

Beats, as of flesh and blood; and, since I saw thee,

Th' affliction of my mind amends, with which,

I fear, a madness held me. This must crave-

An if this be at all-a most strange story.

Thy dukedom I resign, and do entreat

Thou pardon me my wrongs. But how should Prospero

Be living and be here?

PROSPERO. First, noble friend,

Let me embrace thine age, whose honour cannot

Be measur'd or confin'd.

GONZALO. Whether this be

  Or be not, I'll not swear.

  PROSPERO. You do yet taste

  Some subtleties o' th' isle, that will not let
you

  Believe things certain. Welcome, my friends
all!

  *[Aside to SEBASTIAN and ANTONIO] But you,
my brace of*

   lords, were I so minded,

  I here could pluck his Highness' frown upon
you,

  And justify you traitors; at this time

  I will tell no tales.

  SEBASTIAN. [Aside] The devil speaks in him.

  PROSPERO. No.

  For you, most wicked sir, whom to call
brother

  Would even infect my mouth, I do forgive

  Thy rankest fault-all of them; and require

My dukedom of thee, which perforce I know

Thou must restore.

ALONSO. If thou beest Prospero,

Give us particulars of thy preservation;

How thou hast met us here, whom three

hours since

Were wreck'd upon this shore; where I have

lost-

How sharp the point of this remembrance

is!-

My dear son Ferdinand.

PROSPERO. I am woe for't, sir.

ALONSO. Irreparable is the loss; and patience

Says it is past her cure.

PROSPERO. I rather think

You have not sought her help, of whose soft

grace

For the like loss I have her sovereign aid,

And rest myself content.

ALONSO. You the like loss!

PROSPERO. As great to me as late; and, supportable

To make the dear loss, have I means much weaker

Than you may call to comfort you, for I

Have lost my daughter.

ALONSO. A daughter!

O heavens, that they were living both in Naples,

The King and Queen there! That they were, I wish

Myself were mudded in that oozy bed

Where my son lies. When did you lose your daughter?

PROSPERO. In this last tempest. I perceive these lords

At this encounter do so much admire

That they devour their reason, and scarce think

Their eyes do offices of truth, their words

Are natural breath; but, howsoe'er you have

Been justled from your senses, know for
certain

That I am Prospero, and that very duke

Which was thrust forth of Milan; who most
strangely

Upon this shore, where you were wrecked,
was landed

To be the lord on't. No more yet of this;

For 'tis a chronicle of day by day,

Not a relation for a breakfast, nor

Befitting this first meeting. Welcome, sir;

This cell's my court; here have I few
attendants,

And subjects none abroad; pray you, look in.

My dukedom since you have given me again,

I will requite you with as good a thing;

At least bring forth a wonder, to content ye

As much as me my dukedom.

Here PROSPERO discovers FERDINAND and
MIRANDA, playing at chess

MIRANDA. Sweet lord, you play me false.

FERDINAND. No, my dearest love,

　I would not for the world.

MIRANDA. Yes, for a score of kingdoms you
should wrangle

　And I would call it fair play.

ALONSO. If this prove

　A vision of the island, one dear son

　Shall I twice lose.

SEBASTIAN. A most high miracle!

FERDINAND. Though the seas threaten, they
are merciful;

　I have curs'd them without cause.

　　　　　[Kneels]

ALONSO. Now all the blessings

　Of a glad father compass thee about!

　Arise, and say how thou cam'st here.

MIRANDA. O, wonder!

How many goodly creatures are there here!

How beauteous mankind is! O brave new world

That has such people in't!

PROSPERO. 'Tis new to thee.

ALONSO. What is this maid with whom thou wast at play?

Your eld'st acquaintance cannot be three hours;

Is she the goddess that hath sever'd us,

And brought us thus together?

FERDINAND. Sir, she is mortal;

But by immortal Providence she's mine.

I chose her when I could not ask my father

For his advice, nor thought I had one. She

Is daughter to this famous Duke of Milan,

Of whom so often I have heard renown

But never saw before; of whom I have

Receiv'd a second life; and second father

This lady makes him to me.

ALONSO. I am hers.

But, O, how oddly will it sound that I

Must ask my child forgiveness!

PROSPERO. There, sir, stop;

Let us not burden our remembrances with

A heaviness that's gone.

GONZALO. I have inly wept,

Or should have spoke ere this. Look down, you gods,

And on this couple drop a blessed crown;

For it is you that have chalk'd forth the way

Which brought us hither.

ALONSO. I say, Amen, Gonzalo!

GONZALO. Was Milan thrust from Milan, that his issue

Should become Kings of Naples? O, rejoice

Beyond a common joy, and set it down

With gold on lasting pillars: in one voyage

Did Claribel her husband find at Tunis;

And Ferdinand, her brother, found a wife

Where he himself was lost; Prospero his dukedom

In a poor isle; and all of us ourselves

When no man was his own.

ALONSO. [To FERDINAND and MIRANDA] Give me your hands.

Let grief and sorrow still embrace his heart

That doth not wish you joy.

GONZALO. Be it so. Amen!

Re-enter ARIEL, with the MASTER and
BOATSWAIN amazedly following

O look, sir; look, sir! Here is more of us!

I prophesied, if a gallows were on land,

This fellow could not drown. Now, blasphemy,

That swear'st grace o'erboard, not an oath on shore?

Hast thou no mouth by land? What is the news?

  BOATSWAIN. The best news is that we have safely found

    Our King and company; the next, our ship-

    Which but three glasses since we gave out split-

    Is tight and yare, and bravely rigg'd, as when

    We first put out to sea.

  ARIEL. [Aside to PROSPERO] Sir, all this service

    Have I done since I went.

  PROSPERO. [Aside to ARIEL] My tricksy spirit!

  ALONSO. These are not natural events; they strengthen

    From strange to stranger. Say, how came you hither?

  BOATSWAIN. If I did think, sir, I were well awake,

I'd strive to tell you. We were dead of sleep,
     And-how, we know not-all clapp'd under
hatches;
     Where, but even now, with strange and
several noises
     Of roaring, shrieking, howling, jingling
chains,
     And moe diversity of sounds, all horrible,
     We were awak'd; straightway at liberty;
     Where we, in all her trim, freshly beheld
     Our royal, good, and gallant ship; our master
     Cap'ring to eye her. On a trice, so please you,
     Even in a dream, were we divided from
them,
     And were brought moping hither.
  ARIEL. [Aside to PROSPERO] Was't well
done?
  PROSPERO. [Aside to ARIEL] Bravely, my
diligence. Thou shalt be free.

ALONSO. This is as strange a maze as e'er
men trod;

And there is in this business more than
nature

Was ever conduct of. Some oracle

Must rectify our knowledge.

PROSPERO. Sir, my liege,

Do not infest your mind with beating on

The strangeness of this business; at pick'd
leisure,

Which shall be shortly, single I'll resolve you,

Which to you shall seem probable, of every

These happen'd accidents; till when, be
cheerful

And think of each thing well. [Aside to
ARIEL] Come hither, spirit;

Set Caliban and his companions free;

Untie the spell. [Exit ARIEL] How fares my
gracious sir?

There are yet missing of your company

Some few odd lads that you remember not.

Re-enter ARIEL, driving in CALIBAN,
STEPHANO, and

TRINCULO, in their stolen apparel

STEPHANO. Every man shift for all the rest, and let no man take care for himself; for all is but fortune. Coragio, bully-monster, coragio!

TRINCULO. If these be true spies which I wear in my head, here's a goodly sight.

CALIBAN. O Setebos, these be brave spirits indeed!

How fine my master is! I am afraid

He will chastise me.

SEBASTIAN. Ha, ha!

What things are these, my lord Antonio?

Will money buy 'em?

ANTONIO. Very like; one of them

Is a plain fish, and no doubt marketable.

PROSPERO. Mark but the badges of these men, my lords,

Then say if they be true. This mis-shapen knave-

His mother was a witch, and one so strong

That could control the moon, make flows and ebbs,

And deal in her command without her power.

These three have robb'd me; and this demi-devil-

For he's a bastard one-had plotted with them

To take my life. Two of these fellows you

Must know and own; this thing of darkness I

Acknowledge mine.

CALIBAN. I shall be pinch'd to death.

ALONSO. Is not this Stephano, my drunken butler?

SEBASTIAN. He is drunk now; where had he wine?

ALONSO. And Trinculo is reeling ripe; where should they

Find this grand liquor that hath gilded 'em?

How cam'st thou in this pickle?

TRINCULO. I have been in such a pickle since I saw you last that, I fear me, will never out of my bones. I shall not fear fly-blowing.

SEBASTIAN. Why, how now, Stephano!

STEPHANO. O, touch me not; I am not Stephano, but a cramp.

PROSPERO. You'd be king o' the isle, sirrah?

STEPHANO. I should have been a sore one, then.

ALONSO. [Pointing to CALIBAN] This is as strange a thing as e'er I look'd on.

PROSPERO. He is as disproportioned in his manners

As in his shape. Go, sirrah, to my cell;

Take with you your companions; as you look

To have my pardon, trim it handsomely.

CALIBAN. Ay, that I will; and I'll be wise

hereafter,

And seek for grace. What a thrice-double ass

Was I to take this drunkard for a god,

And worship this dull fool!

PROSPERO. Go to; away!

ALONSO. Hence, and bestow your luggage

where you found it.

SEBASTIAN. Or stole it, rather.

Exeunt CALIBAN, STEPHANO, and

TRINCULO

PROSPERO. Sir, I invite your Highness and

your train

To my poor cell, where you shall take your

rest

For this one night; which, part of it, I'll waste

With such discourse as, I not doubt, shall

make it

Go quick away-the story of my life,

And the particular accidents gone by

Since I came to this isle. And in the morn

I'll bring you to your ship, and so to Naples,

Where I have hope to see the nuptial

Of these our dear-belov'd solemnized,

And thence retire me to my Milan, where

Every third thought shall be my grave.

ALONSO. I long

To hear the story of your life, which must

Take the ear strangely.

PROSPERO. I'll deliver all;

And promise you calm seas, auspicious gales,

And sail so expeditious that shall catch

Your royal fleet far off. [Aside to ARIEL] My Ariel, chick,

That is thy charge. Then to the elements

Be free, and fare thou well!-Please you, draw near.

Exeunt

EPILOGUE

EPILOGUE

Spoken by PROSPERO

Now my charms are all o'erthrown,

And what strength I have's mine own,

Which is most faint. Now 'tis true,

I must be here confin'd by you,

Or sent to Naples. Let me not,

Since I have my dukedom got,

And pardon'd the deceiver, dwell

In this bare island by your spell;

But release me from my bands

With the help of your good hands.

Gentle breath of yours my sails

Must fill, or else my project fails,

Which was to please. Now I want

Spirits to enforce, art to enchant;

And my ending is despair

Unless I be reliev'd by prayer,

Which pierces so that it assaults

Mercy itself, and frees all faults.

As you from crimes would pardon'd be,

Let your indulgence set me free.

THE END.